SCHOLASTIC CANADA

BOOK OF LISTS

James Buckley, Jr. and Robert Stremme
with Pat Hancock

Scholastic Canada Ltd.
Toronto New York London Auckland Sydney
Mexico City New Delhi Hong Kong Buenos Aires

Produced by Shoreline Publishing Group LLC
Santa Barbara, California
www.shorelinepublishing.com
Editorial Director: James Buckley, Jr.
Designed by Tom Carling, Carling Design Inc.
Illustrations by Harry Campbell.
Additional editorial help provided by
Beth Adelman, Nanette Cardon (Index),
Jim Gigliotti, David Fischer, and John Walters.

Special Canadian contributor: Pat Hancock

Thanks to Ken Wright and Elysa Jacobs at Scholastic (USA) and Jennifer MacKinnon of
Scholastic Canada for patiently shepherding this book to completion and enthusiastically
supporting it along the way.

Library and Archives Canada Cataloguing in Publication

Buckley, James, 1963–
        Scholastic Canada book of lists / James Buckley, Jr. and Robert Stremme with Pat
Hancock.
ISBN 0-439-95237-9
        1. Handbooks, vade-mecums, etc.--Juvenile literature.
I. Stremme, Robert II. Hancock, Pat III. Title.
AG106.B82 2005   j031.02   C2005-901034-7

Table of Contents

Introduction

People make them to chart the best-selling books and the top ten hockey teams. Your family makes them to bring home the bacon (and the bread and the milk and all the other groceries). You make them to keep track of your favourite songs or movies. What is everybody making? Lists.

Lists are nothing new. As soon as people started using words, they were using lists to keep track of all sorts of information. Lists keep things in order — they combine a whole pile of information into a handy-dandy format.

Lists are the cereal boxes of information; that is, they're the perfect-size package to contain all sorts of great stuff. You can make lists of things in your pocket, books on your shelves, people in your family, or words that start with *Q*. The alphabet is nothing more than a list of letters. A dictionary is a list of words. A phone book is a list of, well, phone numbers. Even the table of contents to this book is a list: a list of the chapters and pages inside. Whether you know it or not, your name is on dozens of lists, from your classroom attendance list to your doctor's patient list. *The Scholastic Canada Book of Lists* is nothing but page after page of lists. You'll find lists in here for just about every subject you might study in school, and some lists that

(i) before (e) except after (c)

Uno Dos Tres

blew/blue

天

you might want to skip right over (c'mon, opera's not that bad!).

In this book, you'll find lists of everything from Super Bowl winners (page 282) to super bowl-fillers (giant food, that is, on page 262) . . . from muscles for frowns (page 146) to oddly named towns (page 102) . . . from history's best (page 60) to animals that rest (page 238).

Some of these lists won't change a bit from the time we typed them until your grandkids read your tattered copy of this book. The ideals of the Charter of Rights and Freedoms (page 63) are always going to be the same. Some of the lists, however, might change as time goes on. Faster roller coasters (page 229) might be built. New movies will leap into the Top 10 (page 217). And, of course, lots of sports records might be set, as well as new champions crowned.

So, remember to use this book as a starting point, a way to get a leg up on finding information that you need. We couldn't put everything that you might need for your life at home or school in here. There's a different word for a book like that: an encyclopedia!

At the bottom of most of the lists are little fact boxes like this one. Here we'll add a historical fact, a key word or definition, interesting numbers, gross trivia, an insider's secret, or even spring a pop quiz on you!

You're not just a reader of this book, either — you're a list-maker. At the end of each chapter is a blank list for you to fill in names, dates, or other information about some part of your world or yourself. Get started by filling in number 5 on this first list. Have fun!

Five Ways I Can Use This Book

1. Learn the capital of every country in case I ever get on *Jeopardy*.

2. It makes a great pillow.

3. Find out why I need a fast boat to catch a marlin.

4. Discover where juju, zouk, samba, and kodo come from.

5. _____.

Abbreviations Used in This Book

Most of the abbreviations used are for measurements. We're using the metric system, but we're also including, in some places, the Imperial system (read more about both on page 108). Here are some of the abbreviations used for these measurements.

cm	centimetre	km	kilometre	ml	millilitre
ft.	foot	l	litre	yd.	yard
g	gram	lb.	pound	oz.	ounce
in.	inch	m	metre	C	Celsius
kg	kilogram	mi	mile	F	Fahrenheit

CHAPTER ONE

History

Just because stuff happened before you were born doesn't mean it isn't important! So our present to you is a trip to the past.

Ancient
Civilizations

The Fertile Crescent was made up of the land around the Tigris and Euphrates rivers, in what is now known as the Middle East. This area is generally considered to be the birthplace of ancient civilizations. However, people on other continents were establishing cultures that would become civilizations, too. Here are some of the world's oldest civilizations.

CIVILIZATION	AREA	DATES*
Sumerian	Fertile Crescent	3500–2000 B.C.
Indus Valley	India	3000–1500 B.C.
Minoan	Crete	3000–1100 B.C.
Egyptian	Egypt	2850–715 B.C.
Hsia	China	2200–1760 B.C.
Babylonian (old)	Mesopotamia	1800–1686 B.C.
Assyrian	Fertile Crescent	1800–899 B.C.
Hittite	Turkey	1640–1200 B.C.
Shang	China	1500–1122 B.C.
Zhou	China	1123–256 B.C.

The Minoan culture flourished on the island of Crete more than 3,000 years ago. Where is Crete located?

Crete is a Greek island in the Mediterranean Sea.

CIVILIZATION	AREA	DATES*
Phoenician	Fertile Crescent	1100–332 B.C.
Greek	Europe	900–200 B.C.
Celts	Europe	800–500 B.C.
Etruscan	Europe	800–300 B.C.
Babylonian (new)	Mesopotamia	625–539 B.C.
Persian	Iran	559–330 B.C.
Roman	Europe	500 B.C.–300 A.D.
Mauryan	India	321–185
Ch'in	China	221–206
Maya	Yucatán	200–850
Gupta	India	320–500
Ghana	West Africa	700–1200
Chimu	Peru	850–1465
Kanem Bornu	West Africa	800–1800
Toltec	Central America	900–1100

*All dates up to Roman are B.C., which stands for "Before Christ." From Roman onward, the dates are A.D., or "Anno Domini," which means "year of the Lord" in Latin. The Western calendar uses the birth of Jesus Christ as the turning point in "counting" years.

Archeologists believe that aboriginal peoples were living along the Eramosa River near Guelph, ON by 9000 B.C. By 5200 B.C. the Sto:lo people were living alongside the Fraser River near Mission, BC. (Some say they may have been there as early as 9000 B.C.)

Hail Caesar!

The Roman Empire lasted for more than 500 years and was the largest empire the world had ever seen. It stretched from Great Britain in the north to parts of Africa in the south and pretty much everywhere else in between. Heading up this empire was a succession of emperors. When they ruled, they were among the most powerful leaders in history.

Emperor	Reign	Emperor	Reign
Augustus (Octavianus)	27 B.C.–A.D. 14	Gordianus	238–244
Tiberius Caesar	14–37	Philippus Arabicus	244–249
Gaius (Caligula)	37–41	Decius	249–251
Claudius Caesar	41–54	Gallus	251–253
Nero	54–68	Aemilianus	253–253
Galba	68–69	Valerianus	253–260
Otho	69–69	Gallienus	260–268
Vitellius	69–69	Claudius Gothicus	268–270
Vespasianus	69–79	Quintillus	270–270
Titus	79–81	Aurelianus	270–275
Domitianus	81–96	Tacitus	275–276
Nerva	96–98	Florianus	276–276
Trajanus	98–117	Probus	276–282
Hadrianus	117–138	Carus	282–283
Antoninus Pius	138–161	Carinus	283–285
Marcus Aurelius	161–180	Diocletianus	285–305
Commodus	180–192	Galerius	305–311
Pertinax	193–193	Maximinus Daia	311–313
Julianus I	193–193	Licinius	313–324
Severus	193–211	Constantinus I	324–337
Caracalla	211–217	Constantinus II	337–361
Macrinus	217–218	Julianus II	361–363
Elagabalus	218–222	Jovianus	363–364
Severus Alexander	222–235	Valens	364–378
Maximinus Thrax	235–238	Theodosius I	378–395

The life of the Roman emperor could be very dangerous. Julianius I was murdered, Claudius Caesar was poisoned, and Nero committed suicide.

Extinct Countries

How can you lose a country? Check your parents' or grandparents' atlases and you will find the names of countries that you don't recognize. These are countries that once existed, but today have been swallowed up by other countries, or split up into smaller countries, or given new names. Here are some places you can't get a ticket to anymore.

EXTINCT COUNTRY (NEW NAME, IF ANY)

Abu Dhabi
Austro-Hungarian Empire
Basutoland (Lesotho)
Bechuanaland (Botswana)
Biafra
British Honduras (Belize)
Burma (Myanmar)
Ceylon (Sri Lanka)
Czechoslovakia
   (Czech Republic & Slovakia)
Formosa (Taiwan)
Germany, Democratic
   Republic of (Germany)
Germany, Federal Republic
   of (Germany)
Gold Coast (Ghana)
Kampuchea (Cambodia)

EXTINCT COUNTRY (NEW NAME, IF ANY)

Malagasy Republic
   (Madagascar)
Manchuria
Ottoman Empire
East Pakistan (Bangladesh)
West Pakistan (Pakistan)
Persia (Iran)
Prussia
Rhodesia (Zimbabwe)
Siam (Thailand)
Sumatra (Indonesia)
Union of Soviet Socialist
   Republics
Upper Volta (Burkina Faso)
Yugoslavia (Serbia and
   Montenegro)
Zanzibar

When Germany was divided into two nations (East and West Germany), the city of Berlin was divided into East and West Berlin by the 43-km (27-mile) "Berlin Wall." To escape East Berlin, people dug tunnels under the wall, scaled the wall, and even floated in balloons over it. The wall came down in 1989.

Famous Leaders

Throughout time, there have been many people who have ruled countries or empires. Some passed into history with barely a whisper; others dominated their age. Rulers such as these have been among the most important and influential people of all time. Here's a list of some of the most well-known, the dates their reigns began, and where they ruled.

TITLE	BEGAN	AREA RULED OR TITLE
Alexander the Great	332 B.C.	Asia Minor and Egypt
Cleopatra	51 B.C.	Queen of Egypt
Charlemagne	800	Holy Roman Empire
William the Conqueror	1066	Conqueror and King of England
Genghis Khan	1200	Mongolian Empire, much of Asia
Ivan the Great	1462	Russian prince
Henry VIII	1509	King of England
Montezuma II	1519	Aztec ruler in Central America
Elizabeth I	1558	Queen of England
Tokugawa Ieyasu	1603	Shogun of Japan
King Louis XIV, the Sun King	1643	King of France
Peter the Great	1682	Tsar of Russia
Catherine the Great	1762	Empress of Russia
George Washington	1789	First U.S. president
Napoléon Bonaparte	1799	Emperor of France
Simón Bolívar	1810	South American leader
Victoria	1837	Queen of England
Benito Juárez	1858	President of Mexico
Abraham Lincoln	1860	16th U.S. president

TITLE	BEGAN	AREA RULED OR TITLE
Giuseppe Garibaldi	1861	Unified Italy into one country
Sir John A. Macdonald	1867	First prime minister of Canada
Vladimir Lenin	1917	Revolutionary leader of the U.S.S.R.
Mahatma Gandhi	1920	Leader of peaceful revolt in India
Joseph Stalin	1922	Leader of the Soviet Union
Franklin Delano Roosevelt	1932	32nd U.S. president
Adolf Hitler	1933	German dictator; head of Nazis
Mao Tse-tung	1935	Communist leader of China
Winston Churchill	1940	Prime minister of Great Britain
Nikita Khrushchev	1953	Soviet leader
General Charles de Gaulle	1959	President of France
Fidel Castro	1959	Communist leader of Cuba
John F. Kennedy	1960	43rd U.S. president
Golda Meir	1969	Israeli prime minster
Margaret Thatcher	1979	Prime minister of Great Britain
Pierre Elliott Trudeau	1979	Prime minister of Canada
Indira Gandhi	1980	Prime minister of India
Corazon Aquino	1986	President of the Philippines
Lech Walesa	1990	Polish president
Boris Yeltsin	1991	Russian president
Nelson Mandela	1994	South African president

Which of these words or phrases has NOT been used in a country somewhere to describe its leader: Shah, Kaiser, Emperor, Chief, Big Fella, Sultan, Emir, Grand Mufti?

Answer: Unless you count basketball teams as countries, no nation calls its leader "Big Fella." The others are all real, however.

Aboriginal Peoples

First Nations people (North American Indians), Métis, and Inuit are the three main groups of Aboriginal people recognized in Canada's Constitution. The Métis—of mixed European and Aboriginal ancestry—live in most parts of Canada. The Inuit live mainly in Canada's far north, making up about 80 per cent of the population of Nunavut. Here is a list of some First Nations peoples, loosely grouped according to where they live, or once lived when European settlers arrived.

NORTHWEST COAST/PLATEAU

Bella Coola	Lillooet	Tagish
Carrier	Nisga'a	Tahltan
Chilcotin	Nuu-chah-nulth	Thompson
Gitskan	Okanagan	Tlingit
Haida	Salish	Tsimshian
Ktunaxa	Shuswap	

GREAT LAKES/ST. LAWRENCE

Cayuga	Neutral	Potawatomi
Erie	Odawa	Seneca
Huron	Ojibwa	Tobacco
Mohawk	Oneida	Tuscarora
Montagnais	Onandaga	

# of Canada

PLAINS/PRAIRIES

Assiniboine	Chipewyan	Plains Cree
Blackfoot	Gros Venture	Sarcee
Blood	Peigan	Sioux

EAST COAST

| Beothuk | Mi'kmaq | Penebscot |
| Maliseet | Passamaquoddy | |

SUB-ARCTIC

| Dogrib | Kaska | Sekani |
| Hare | Slave | Tutchone |

ARCTIC

| Baffin | Copper | Mackenzie |
| Caribou | Igulik | Netsilik |

The 2001 Canadian census counted 976,305 people who identified themselves as Aboriginal (North American Indian, Métis, or Inuit).

Important Wars

Sad to say, this list could have been much longer. War has been a part of civilization since its earliest days. Wars are key turning points in the course of history. The conflicts listed here had the most long-lasting impact.

WAR	DATES
Peloponnesian War (Greece)	431–404 B.C.
Punic Wars (Rome vs. North Africa)	264–146 B.C.
Norman Invasion of England	1066
Hundred Years' War (France vs. England)	1337–1453
War of the Roses	1455–1485
Thirty Years' War (France vs. England)	1618–1648
English Civil War	1642–1651
American Revolution	1775–1783
Wars of the French Revolution	1789–1799
Napoleonic Wars (France vs. Europe)	1803–1815
War of 1812 (United States vs. Great Britain)	1812–1815
Mexican-American War	1846–1848
Italian War of Independence	1848–1849
American Civil War	1861–1865
Chinese-Japanese War	1894–1895

WAR	DATES
Spanish-American War	1898
Boer War (Great Britain vs. South Africans)	1899–1902
World War I	1914–1918
Spanish Civil War	1936–1939
Chinese-Japanese War	1937–1945
World War II	1939–1945
Israeli War of Independence	1948–1949
Korean War	1950–1953
Cuban Revolution	1953–1959
Vietnam War	1954–1975
Suez War (Israel vs. Egypt)	1956
Six-Day War (Israel vs. Egypt)	1967
Cambodian Civil War	1970–1975
October War (Israel vs. Egypt)	1973
Iran-Iraq War	1980–1988
Persian Gulf War	1990–1991
War in Iraq	2001–

The British fought the French in the Seven Years War (1756-1763). What is the North American part of this war called?

Answer: The French and Indian War.

Famous Explorers

Explorers take on the challenge of discovering the new and unknown areas of our universe. Sometime it is difficult to determine who was first, but these people faced many hardships and trials in order to reach their goals. What's left to explore? The land under the oceans and the vast area of outer space remain mostly unexplored. Where would you want to explore?

EXPLORER, COUNTRY	DATES	AREA EXPLORED
Chang Ch'ien, China	138–109 B.C.	Silk Road trade route through Asia
Hsuan-tsang, China	629–645	India
Erik the Red, Norway	c. 900	Greenland
Leif Eriksson, Norway	c. 1000	Newfoundland
Marco Polo, Italy	1271–1295	Mongolian Empire
Ibn Battuta, Morocco	1325–1354	Africa
Cheng Ho, China	1405–1433	Pacific Islands
Bartolomeu Dias, Portugal	1487–1488	Cape of Good Hope, Africa
Christopher Columbus, Spain	1492–1502	San Salvador, West Indies
John Cabot, Italy/England	1497–1498	Newfoundland
Vasco da Gama, Portugal	1497–1498	India, reached by sea
Amerigo Vespucci, Spain	1497–1502	South America, West Indies
Pedro Cabral, Portugal	1500–1501	Sailed from Africa to India and Brazil
Vasco de Balboa, Spain	1513	Pacific Ocean
Juan Ponce de León, Spain	1513, 1521	Florida
Hernando Cortés, Spain	1519–1521	Mexico
Ferdinand Magellan, Spain	1519–1521	First to sail around the world
Giovanni da Verrazano, Italy	1524, 1528	North American eastern coast

EXPLORER, COUNTRY	DATES	AREA EXPLORED
Pánfilo de Narváez, Spain	1528–1536	Florida, Mexico
Francisco Pizarro, Spain	1531–1533	Peru
Jacques Cartier, France	1535–1541	St. Lawrence River, Canada
Hernando de Soto, Spain	1539–1542	Mississippi River, American Southwest
Francisco de Coronado, Spain	1540–1542	American Southwest
Juan Rodríguez Cabrillo, Spain	1542–1543	California
Sir Francis Drake, England	1577–1580	Sailed around the world
Samuel de Champlain, France	1603–1620	Great Lakes, Quebec
Henry Hudson, England	1607–1611	Hudson River, Hudson Bay
David Thompson, Canada	1797–1811	Western Canada
James Cook, England	1772–1779	Tonga, Easter Island, Hawaii
Lewis & Clark, U.S.	1804–1806	Western United States
Charles Darwin, England	1831–1836	Galápagos Islands, Ecuador
David Livingstone, Scotland	1851, 1855	Victoria Falls, Africa
Matthew Henson, U.S.	1909	Co-discovered North Pole
Robert Peary, U.S.	1909	Co-discovered North Pole
Roald Amundsen, Norway	1911	First person to reach South Pole
Bertram Thomas, England	1930	Crossed Rub' al Khali Desert
Jacques Cousteau, France	1943–1997	Undersea world
Neil Armstrong, U.S.	1969	First person to walk on the moon

David Livingstone discovered Victoria Falls in Africa, but then disappeared. American explorer H. M. Stanley finally located Dr. Livingstone, who had been recovering from an illness with the help of a native tribe. Stanley greeted the "missing" man with the famous phrase, "Dr. Livingstone, I presume."

A Dozen Great Canadians

As this chapter shows, Canada has a long and distinguished history. In 2004 polls were taken among Canadian citizens to choose the nation's important personalities. Here, in alphabetical order, are a dozen men and women of note whose names appeared in those polls.

Louise Arbour (1947-) Canadian Supreme Court Judge and UN High Commissioner for Human Rights

Frederick Banting (1891-1941) Discovered insulin

Roberta Bondar (1945-) First Canadian female astronaut in space

Marguerite Bourgeoys (1620-1700) Canada's first teacher, she is also a co-founder of Montreal

Samuel de Champlain (1570?-1635) Father of New France

Tommy Douglas (1904-1986) Powerful politician, considered the father of Canada's universal health care system

Wayne Gretzky (1961-) Hockey legend

Sir John A. Macdonald (1815-1891) Father of Confederation and Canada's first prime minister

Lester B. Pearson (1897-1972) Canada's 14th prime minister and Nobel Peace Prize winner

Louis Riel (1844-1885) Métis leader and founder of Manitoba

Charles Saunders (1867-1937) Breeder of Marquis wheat that brought prosperity to the Prairies

Pierre Elliott Trudeau (1919-2000) Prime minister when the Official Languages Act, the new Constitution Act, and the Charter of Rights and Freedoms became law

Sir John A. Macdonald's leadership was vital in uniting the French and British parts of what would become Canada. But he was not born in Canada; he moved here when he was five years old. In what country was he born?

Answer: Macdonald was born in Glasgow, Scotland.

Talking About Canada

Here's a list of some memorable sayings by well-known Canadians about Canada and Canadians.

"What has Confederation done for Canada? What has Confederation not done for Canada?"
— EARL GREY

"The greatest good to the greatest number."
— TIMOTHY EATON

"Canada is my kind of country." — DONALD GORDON

"For they looked in the future and what did they see/They saw an iron road runnin' from the sea to the sea..."
— GORDON LIGHTFOOT

"Canada has never been a melting pot; more like a tossed salad."
— ARNOLD EDINBOROUGH

"Living next to you [the U.S.] is in some ways like sleeping with an elephant. No matter how friendly or even-tempered is the beast...one is affected by every twitch and grunt."
— PIERRE ELLIOTT TRUDEAU

"A society which emphasizes uniformity is one which creates intolerance and hate."
— PIERRE ELLIOTT TRUDEAU

"If some countries have too much history, we have too much geography."
— WILLIAM LYON MACKENZIE KING

"Make peace as exciting as war." — JOHN GRIERSON

What well-known Canadian said this about his day at the "office": "How would you like a job where, if you make a mistake, a big red light goes on and 18,000 people boo?"

Answer: Jacques Plante, star hockey goaltender

Building Canada

Canada was settled by Europeans from England and France and other countries, beginning in the 1500s. Eventually, all those settlers began to band together to turn their collection of small settlements into a nation. Here are the steps they went through to become the continent-spanning nation of today.

1758 Nova Scotia gets an elected assembly, the first elected assembly in a British colony

1759 The British defeat the French in Quebec, and Canada becomes a British colony

1773 Prince Edward Island gets an elected assembly

1784 New Brunswick becomes a separate colony from Nova Scotia, with its own elected assembly

1791 The Constitutional Act divides Canada into Upper Canada (now Ontario) and Lower Canada (now Quebec), each with an elected assembly

1832 Newfoundland gets an elected assembly

1837-38 Rebellions in Ontario and Quebec attempt to make the two provinces' appointed executive councils answerable to the elected assemblies

1841 The Union Act unites Upper and Lower Canada into the province of Canada, with one elected legislature made up of equal numbers of representatives from Canada East (Quebec) and Canada West (Ontario)

1848 New Brunswick, Nova Scotia, and the province of Canada each get responsible government, with the executive being responsible to the elected assembly

1851 Prince Edward Island gets responsible government

1855 Newfoundland gets responsible government

1867 The British North America Act creates the new Dominion of Canada, with responsible government at the federal level, and with the first provinces to join Confederation keeping their separate responsible governments at the provincial level

1867 New Brunswick, Nova Scotia, Ontario, and Quebec join Confederation.

1870 Manitoba and the Northwest Territories join Confederation

1871 British Columbia joins Confederation

1873 Prince Edward Island joins Confederation

1898 Yukon Territory joins Confederation

1905 Saskatchewan and Alberta join Confederation

1949 Newfoundland joins Confederation

1999 The territory of Nunavut joins Confederation

PsSST The 1982 Canadian Charter of Rights and Freedoms was another important step in building Canada today. See more on page 63.

Canada's Prime Ministers

The office of prime minister was established in 1867 when Canada became a confederation. John A. Macdonald (later Sir John) was the first prime minister. He was the leader of the Liberal-Conservative Party and an experienced politician. Today the "P.M.," as he or she is sometimes known, is the leader of the political party that has a majority or leadership role in parliament. Prime ministers are also, by tradition, holders of a seat in the House of Commons (see page 55).

NAME	YEARS IN OFFICE
Paul Martin	2003–
Jean Chrétien	1993–2003
Kim Campbell	1993
Brian Mulroney	1984–1993
John Turner	1984
Pierre Trudeau	1980–1984
Joe Clark	1979–1980
Pierre Trudeau	1968–1979
Lester B. Pearson	1963–1968
John Diefenbaker	1957–1963
Louis St. Laurent	1948–1957
W.L. Mackenzie King	1935–1948

NAME	YEARS IN OFFICE
Richard Bennett	1930–1935
W.L. Mackenzie King	1926–1930
Arthur Meighen	1926
W.L. Mackenzie King	1921–1926
Arthur Meighen	1920–1921
Robert Borden	1911–1920
Wilfrid Laurier	1896–1911
Charles Tupper	1896
Mackenzie Bowell	1894–1896
John Thompson	1892–1894
John Abbott	1891–1892
John A. Macdonald	1878–1891
Alexander Mackenzie	1873–1878
John A. Macdonald	1867–1873

At **21 years in office, W.L. Mackenzie King** was Canada's longest-serving prime minister. He is followed in the ranks by **Wilfrid Laurier** and **Pierre Trudeau**, who each served as prime minister for **15 years.**

Governors General

Governors general are appointed by the monarch of Great Britain. The office was established as part of the 1867 re-organization of Canada. The governor general's role in government has declined over time. While once it was a very powerful post, today its role is more advisory or ceremonial, as Canada has become independent from Great Britain.

GOVERNOR GENERAL	YEAR TERM BEGAN
Michaëlle Jean	2005
Adrienne Clarkson	1999
Roméo LeBlanc	1995
Ramon John Hnatyshyn	1990
Jeanne Sauvé	1984
Edward Richard Schreyer	1979
Jules Léger	1974
Daniel Roland Michener	1967
Georges Philias Vanier	1959
Vincent Massey	1952

Thanks, Baron!

The governor general whose name is most well-known around the world is probably Baron (later Lord) Stanley. But he's not famous for his work in government. Instead, he's better known as the person who donated the hockey championship trophy that today is known as the Stanley Cup. He donated the silver cup in 1893 to be given to the national amateur hockey champion. From 1926 onward, it was given to the champion of the National Hockey League. It is the oldest trophy in pro sports.

GOVERNOR GENERAL	YEAR TERM BEGAN
Viscount Alexander	1946
Earl of Athlone	1940
Baron Tweedsmuir of Elsfield	1935
Earl of Bessborough	1931
Viscount Willingdon	1926
Lord Byng of Vimy	1921
Duke of Devonshire	1916
Duke of Connaught	1911
Earl Grey	1904
Earl of Minto	1898
Earl of Aberdeen	1893
Baron Stanley of Preston	1888
Marquess of Landsdowne	1883
Duke of Argyll	1878
Earl of Dufferin	1872
Lord Lisgar	1869
Viscount Monck	1867

Jeanne Sauvé was the first female governor general in Canada's history. A former member of Parliament, she was also a successful journalist. As an MP and governor general, she helped spearhead important youth programs that continue to benefit Canadians.

U.S. Presidents and Vice Presidents

Hail to the Chiefs

He (and it's always been a he . . . so far!) is the United States of America's commander in chief, is the head of the executive branch, and holds one of the most powerful offices in the world. The rules: a person who wants to become president must be at least 35 years old and born in the United States.

PRESIDENT	VICE PRESIDENT	POLITICAL PARTY	YEARS
1. George Washington	John Adams	Federalist	1789–1797
2. John Adams	Thomas Jefferson	Federalist	1797–1801
3. Thomas Jefferson	Aaron Burr	Dem.-Rep.*	1801–1805
	George Clinton	Dem.-Rep.*	1805–1809
4. James Madison	George Clinton	Dem.-Rep.*	1809–1817
5. James Monroe	Daniel D. Tompkins	Dem.-Rep.*	1817–1825
6. John Quincy Adams	John C. Calhoun	Dem.-Rep.*	1825–1829
7. Andrew Jackson	John C. Calhoun	Democrat	1829–1833
	Martin Van Buren	Democrat	1833–1837
8. Martin Van Buren	Richard M. Johnson	Democrat	1837–1841
9. William H. Harrison	John Tyler	Whig	1841
10. John Tyler		Whig	1841–1845
11. James K. Polk	George M. Dallas	Democrat	1845–1849
12. Zachary Taylor	Millard Fillmore	Whig	1849–1850
13. Millard Fillmore		Whig	1850–1853
14. Franklin Pierce	William R. King	Democrat	1853–1857
15. James Buchanan	John C. Breckenridge	Democrat	1857–1861
16. Abraham Lincoln	Hannibal Hamlin	Republican	1861–1865
	Andrew Johnson	Republican	1865
17. Andrew Johnson		Union	1865–1869
18. Ulysses S. Grant	Schuyler Colfax	Republican	1869–1873
	Henry Wilson	Republican	1873–1877
19. Rutherford B. Hayes	William A. Wheeler	Republican	1877–1881
20. James Garfield	Chester A. Arthur	Republican	1881
21. Chester A. Arthur		Republican	1881–1885

PRESIDENT	VICE PRESIDENT	POLITICAL PARTY	YEARS
22. Grover Cleveland	Thomas A. Hendricks	Democrat	1885–1889
23. Benjamin Harrison	Levi P. Morton	Republican	1889–1893
24. Grover Cleveland	Adlai E. Stevenson	Democrat	1893–1897
25. William McKinley	Garret A. Hobart	Republican	1897–1901
	Theodore Roosevelt	Republican	1901
26. Theodore Roosevelt		Republican	1901–1905
	Charles W. Fairbanks	Republican	1905–1909
27. William H. Taft	James S. Sherman	Republican	1909–1913
28. Woodrow Wilson	Thomas R. Marshall	Democrat	1913–1921
29. Warren G. Harding	Calvin Coolidge	Republican	1921–1923
30. Calvin Coolidge		Republican	1923–1925
	Charles G. Dawes	Republican	1925–1929
31. Herbert C. Hoover	Charles Curtis	Republican	1929–1933
32. Franklin D. Roosevelt	John N. Garner	Democrat	1933–1941
	Henry A. Wallace	Democrat	1941–1945
	Harry S. Truman	Democrat	1945
33. Harry S. Truman		Democrat	1945–1949
	Albert W. Barkley	Democrat	1949–1953
34. Dwight D. Eisenhower	Richard M. Nixon	Republican	1953–1961
35. John F. Kennedy	Lyndon B. Johnson	Democrat	1961–1963
36. Lyndon B. Johnson		Democrat	1963–1965
	Hubert H. Humphrey	Democrat	1965–1969
37. Richard M. Nixon	Spiro T. Agnew	Republican	1969–1973
	Gerald R. Ford	Republican	1973–1974
38. Gerald R. Ford	Nelson A. Rockefeller	Republican	1974–1977
39. James E. Carter, Jr.	Walter F. Mondale	Democrat	1977–1981
40. Ronald Reagan	George Bush	Republican	1981–1989
41. George Bush	J. Danforth Quayle	Republican	1989–1993
42. William J. Clinton	Albert Gore	Democrat	1993–2001
43. George W. Bush	Richard Cheney	Republican	2001–

* Oddly, an early political party was called "Democratic-Republican." Those names were later used for separate parties.

George Washington, the first president, chose what Americans call their chief executive. Not Your Honour or Your Majesty — just "Mr. President."

Famous Women in History

She's in Charge

Many important women in world history are remembered for political work. Other women on this list are remembered for being pioneers in a certain area, opening the way for many more women to follow.

NAME, TITLE	LIFE SPAN
Nefertiti, Queen of Egypt	14th century B.C.
Cleopatra, Queen of Egypt	69–30 B.C.
Eleanor of Aquitaine, Queen of England and France	1122–1204
Joan of Arc, Leader of French army	1412–1431
Isabella I, Queen of Spain	1451–1504
Catherine de Medici, Queen of France	1519–1589
Elizabeth I, Queen of England	1533–1603
Mbande Nzinga, Queen of Ndongo and Matamba*	1582–1663
Catherine the Great, Empress of Russia	1729–1796
Marie Antoinette, Queen of France	1755–1793
Elizabeth Cady Stanton, Founder, Woman Suffrage Assoc.#	1815–1902
Victoria, Queen of England	1819–1901
Susan B. Anthony, Founder, Woman Suffrage Assoc.	1820–1906
Clara Barton, Founder, American Red Cross	1821–1912
Mother Jones, Famous labour leader	1830–1930

NAME, TITLE	LIFE SPAN
Tz'u-hsi, Dowager empress of China	1835–1908
Liliuokalani, Queen of Hawaii	1838–1917
Nancy Astor, First woman in British Parliament	1879–1964
Jeannette Rankin, First woman member, U.S. Congress	1880–1973
Agnes C. Macphail, First woman, Canadian Parliament	1890–1954
Amelia Earhart, First female pilot to cross Atlantic	1897–1937
Golda Meir, Prime Minister of Israel	1898–1978
Ellen Fairclough, First female Canadian cabinet minister	1905–2004
Rachel Carson, Environmental scientist and activist	1907–1964
Mother Teresa, Founder, Missionaries of Charity	1910–1997
Indira Gandhi, Prime Minister of India	1917–1984
Margaret Thatcher, Prime Minister of England	1925–
Elizabeth II, Queen of Great Britain	1926–
Bertha Wilson, First female, Supreme Court of Canada	1926–
Rita Johnston, First female Canadian premier	1935–
Audrey McLaughlin, First woman leader, Canadian political party	1936–

* Former kingdom in Africa; # This group fought for women's right to vote in the U.S.

PsSST

The first female prime minister of Canada was Kim Campbell, who took office in 1993. She was also Canada's first female Minister of Justice and Attorney General.

More Than Just Words

Today we get our big news from TV, the radio, or the Internet. Throughout history, however, some of the biggest news has been made by important books or documents. Here is a list of some influential documents or books.

The Republic (360 B.C.)
Greek philosopher Plato's thoughts on government and more.

Magna Carta (1215)
Signed by England's King John and British noblemen, it helped pave the way for democracy many years later.

Principia Mathematica (1687)
Sir Isaac Newton laid out some of the basics of mathematics, gravity, and physics.

Declaration of Independence (1776)
The United States declared itself free from British rule.

U.S. Constitution (1787)
Along with the ten-amendment Bill of Rights, this set up the basics of American government.

Communist Manifesto (1848)
Written by Karl Marx and Friedrich Engels, it spelled out a social philosophy later used to help form the Soviet Union.

The Origin of Species (1859)
Scientist Charles Darwin described the theory of evolution for the first time.

Constitution Act (1867)
This important piece of legislation formed the basis for modern Canada, establishing a federal government.

Charter of Rights and Freedoms (1982)
Formally established a series of personal rights in Canada.

The Bible and the Koran (also spelled Qur'an) have also played vital roles in shaping history. The Bible's Old Testament contains the holy book of Judaism, while the entire Bible is scripture for Christianity. The Koran is the holy book of Islam.

Internet Timeline

The Internet dates back to the 1960s, when ARPA (the U.S. Defense Department's Advanced Research Projects Agency) linked university computers together. This "network" let computers in many places talk to one another. Of course, today, the Internet is about people connecting, not just computers. Here is a timeline showing the development of the Internet and the programs and machines it needs to work.

1946 ENIAC—first electronic computer created

1951 Ferranti Mark I—first commercially produced computer

1969 ARPANET created; grows to 15 sites in two years

1971 First e-mail sent by engineer Ray Tomlinson in Connecticut

1973 Transmission Control Protocol/Internet Protocol (TCP/IP) designed; lets computers communicate over the Internet

1981 IBM PC introduced

1984 Macintosh introduced

1989 Silicon memory chips introduced

1990 World Wide Web invented

1993 Mosaic, first graphic Web browser, released

1994 Netscape Navigator browser released

1996 45,000,000+ people using the Internet worldwide

1999 150,000,000+ people using the Internet worldwide

1999 "Melissa" virus infects computers via e-mail, followed by the "Love Bug" virus in 2000

2001 36,000,000+ Internet domain names registered

2001 Napster ordered to stop distributing copyrighted music

2002 You use the Web to talk to your friends and buy stuff

2004 iTunes Music Store opens to sell digital music

Save time chatting on the Web with these easy shortcuts: **PLS** (please); **LOL** (laugh out loud); **ROTFL** (rolling on the floor laughing); **BTW** (by the way); **HHOK** (ha, ha, only kidding); **TYVM** (thank you very much).

Who Named What?

Archaeological evidence shows that the ancestors of today's First Nations and Inuit peoples were exploring "Canada" as early as 20,000 years ago, but there's no written record of which of them got where first. So, some places in Canada are named after the European explorers who "discovered" these places—which, of course, had been there all along!

Baffin Island
William Baffin (1584–1622), British Arctic explorer

Cabot Strait
John Cabot (1450?–1499), Italian-born English explorer

Fraser River
Simon Fraser (1776–1862) American-born Canadian explorer and fur trader

Frobisher Bay*
Martin Frobisher (1535? –1594), English explorer and privateer

Hudson Bay
Henry Hudson (1565?–1611?), English arctic explorer

James Bay
Thomas James (1593–1635?), English explorer

Mackenzie River
Alexander Mackenzie (1764–1820), Scottish-born explorer and fur trader

Strait of Juan de Fuca
Juan de Fuca (1536? –1602?), Greek-born Spanish navigator

Thompson River
David Thompson (1770–1857), English-born mapmaker and surveyor

Vancouver Island
George Vancouver (1757–1798), English naval officer and explorer

PSSST

*In 1987, the name of Frobisher Bay—the settlement, not the water—was changed from the explorer's name to the Native place name, Iqaluit. Iqaluit means "place of fish" in Inuktitut.

World Heritage Sites

The United Nations Educational, Scientific, and Cultural Organization (UNESCO) works to preserve hundreds of natural and cultural places. These sites each have such special value they should be protected so future generations can appreciate and enjoy them. The nearly 800 sites on the World Heritage list include the Pyramids in Egypt, the Galapagos Islands in Ecuador, and Grand Canyon National Park and the Statue of Liberty in the United States. Here's a partial list of the UNESCO World Heritage sites in Canada.

SITE	PROVINCE(S)
Canadian Rocky Mountain Parks	AB/BC
Dinosaur Provincial Park	AB
Gros Morne National Park	NL
Head-Smashed-In Buffalo Jump	AB
Historic District of Quebec	QC
L'Anse aux Meadows Historic Site	NL
Miguasha Park	QC
Nahanni National Park Reserve	NT
Old Town Lunenburg	NS
SGaang Gwaii*	BC
Waterton Glacier International Peace Park	AB/MT
Wood Buffalo National Park	AB/NT

*Formerly Anthony Island

PsSST

Kluane/Wrangell (YT)-St. Elias/Glacier Bay (Alaska)-Tatshenshini-Alsek (BC) are four national parks that taken all together form the largest internationally protected UNESCO Heritage site in the world.

Fabulous Female Firsts

Being the first woman to do a job that only men had done before took courage. Some men resented women who tried to do such a thing and made their lives very difficult. Other women also disapproved of these pioneering females. Here's a list of some Canadian women who worked hard to become the first females in their chosen professions.

1867 Emily Howard Stowe First Canadian woman to practice medicine openly (wasn't given a licence until 1880)

1875 Grace Lockhart First female university graduate in Canada and the British Empire (a degree from New Brunswick's Mount Allison University)

1875 Jennie Trout First woman licensed to practise medicine in Canada (trained in the United States)

1881 Augusta Stowe Gullen First woman to receive a medical degree from a Canadian university

1897 Clara Brett Martin First female lawyer in Canada and the British empire

1898 C.L. Josephine Wells Canada's first woman dentist

1912 Carrie Derick First woman to be become a full university professor in Canada

1916 Emily Murphy First female magistrate in Canada and the British empire

1920 Marjorie Hill Canada's first female architect

1921 Mary Ellen Smith First woman cabinet minister in Canada and the British empire

1927 Elsie Gregory MacGill First woman in Canada to graduate in engineering

In 1988, nine-year-old Emma Houlston became the youngest person to ever fly a plane across Canada. Emma's flight began in Victoria, BC. She flew three hours a day, and landed in St. John's, NL two weeks later.

Obscure Famous People

Over the years, some people who were at one time world-famous have faded from view. Although they were once well-known celebrities around the world, the men and women on this list are often forgotten today.

PERSON, LIFE SPAN/ACHIEVEMENT

Nellie Bly, 1864–1922
In 1890, this pioneering journalist travelled around the world in 72 days.

Howard Carter, 1874–1939
In 1922, Carter uncovered the tomb of the ancient Egyptian King Tut.

Douglas "Wrong Way" Corrigan, 1907–1995
In 1938, Corrigan made headlines when he filed a flight plan to fly from Brooklyn to California — but ended up in Ireland!

Louis Cyr, 1863–1912
In the 1890s Quebec-born Louis Cyr was well-known as the strongest man in the world. He once lifted 1869 kg (4112 lb.) on his back.

Florence Nightingale Graham, 1880?–1966
Graham changed her name to Elizabeth Arden when she opened a beauty parlour and began selling cosmetics. She was the first to market makeovers.

Pauline Johnson (aka Tekahionwake), 1861–1913
Daughter of a Mohawk chief, Johnson was a very popular writer and performer whose poetry recitals attracted large audiences in North America and Europe.

William Osler, 1849–1919
Canadian William Osler was the 20th century's most famous physician. A brilliant doctor, he was also one of the world's best teachers of medicine.

Major Taylor, 1878–1932
In the late 1890s, this bicycle racer was the most famous athlete in the world. He was also the first African-American pro athlete.

PsSST

Why was **William Osler** such a pioneer in teaching medicine? He often moved his students out of classrooms and into patients' rooms. His "bedside" teaching methods became the standard for all medical schools.

My Family Tree

No, it's not the one in the backyard. Your family tree is a list of all of your relatives, going as far back as you can. Start with your mother and father and siblings, if you have any, then work your way backward in time.

Father: _____ Mother: _____

Siblings (brothers and sisters):

_____ _____

_____ _____

Father's parents:

_____ _____

Mother's parents:

_____ _____

Father's siblings:

_____ _____

_____ _____

Mother's siblings:

_____ _____

_____ _____

Father's parents' siblings:

_____ _____

Mother's parents' siblings:

_____ _____

Father's grandparents:

_____ _____

Mother's grandparents:

_____ _____

CHAPTER TWO

Social Studies

There's something for everyone in social studies. Whether you need to find the capital of Mongolia, the definition of plutocracy, the inventor of chocolate chips (thanks to whoever that is!), or why the Colossus was so "wonder"-ful, you'll find it in this chapter.

Countries

The number of countries in the world is always changing, as some larger countries break up into smaller ones, or former colonies become independent states. The two newest members of this list of countries are East Timor (2002) and Serbia and Montenegro (2002).

COUNTRY/CAPITAL	MAIN LANGUAGES	CURRENCY
Afghanistan/Kabul	Pushtu, Dari Persian, Turkic languages	Afghani
Albania/Tiranë	Albanian, Greek	Lek
Algeria/Algiers	Arabic, French, Berber dialects	Dinar
Andorra/Andorra la Vella	Catalan, French, Spanish	Euro
Angola/Luanda	Bantu, Portuguese	Kwanza
Antigua and Barbuda/Saint John's	English	East Caribbean dollar
Argentina/Buenos Aires	Spanish, English, Italian, German	Peso
Armenia/Yerevan	Armenian, Russian	Dram
Australia/Canberra	English	Australian dollar
Austria/Vienna	German	Euro
Azerbaijan/Baku	Azerbaijani Turkic, Russian, Armenian	Manat
Bahamas/Nassau	English, Creole	Bahamian dollar
Bahrain/Manama	Arabic, English, Farsi, Urdu	Bahrain dinar
Bangladesh/Dhaka	Bangla, English	Taka
Barbados/Bridgetown	English	Barbados dollar
Belarus/Minsk	Belorussian	Belorussian ruble
Belgium/Brussels	Dutch, French, German	Euro
Belize/Belmopan	English, Creole, Spanish, Garifuna	Belize dollar
Benin/Porto-Norvo	French	Franc CFA
Bhutan/Thimphu	Dzongkha	Ngultrum
Bolivia/La Paz, Sucre	Spanish, Quechua, Aymara, Guarani	Boliviano
Bosnia and Herzegovina/Sarajevo	Serbian, Croatian	Dinar
Botswana/Gaborone	English, Setswana	Pula
Brazil/Brasília	Portuguese	Real
Brunei/Bandar Seri Begawan	Malay, English, Chinese	Brunei dollar
Bulgaria/Sofia	Bulgarian	Lev
Burkina Faso/Ouagadougou	French, tribal languages	Franc
Burundi/Bujumbura	Kirundi, French, Swahili	Burundi franc

of the World

COUNTRY/CAPITAL	MAIN LANGUAGES	CURRENCY
Cambodia/Phnom Penh	Khmer, French, English	Rial
Cameroon/Yaoundé	French, English, tribal languages	Franc CFA
Canada/Ottawa	English, French	Canadian dollar
Cape Verde/Praia	Portuguese, Crioulo	Cape Verdean escudo
Central African Republic/Bangui	French, Sangho, Arabic, Swahili	Franc CFA
Chad/N'Djamena	French, Arabic	Franc CFA
Chile/Santiago	Spanish	Peso
China/Beijing	Chinese, Mandarin	Yuan
Colombia/Bogotá	Spanish	Peso
Comoros/Moroni	French, Arabic	Franc CFA
Congo, Dem. Rep. of the/Kinshasa	French, Swahili, Ishiluba, Kikongo	Congolese franc
Congo, Republic of the/Brazzaville	French, Lingala, Kikongo	Franc CFA
Costa Rica/San José	Spanish	Colón
Croatia/Zagreb	Serbian, Croatian	Kuna
Cuba/Havana	Spanish	Peso
Cyprus/Lefkosia (Nicosia)	Greek, Turkish, English	Cyprus pound
Czech Republic/Prague	Czech, Slovak	Koruna
Denmark/Copenhagen	Danish, Faeroese, Greenlandic	Krone
Djibouti/Djibouti	Arabic, French, Somali, Afar	Djibouti franc
Dominica/Roseau	English, French *patois*	East Caribbean dollar
Dominican Republic/Santo Domingo	Spanish, English	Peso
East Timor/Dili	Portugeuse, Indonesian, Tetum	Egyptian pound
Ecuador/Quito	Spanish, Quechua	U.S. dollar
Egypt/Cairo	Arabic, English, French	Egyptian pound
El Salvador/San Salvador	Spanish, Nahua	Colón
Equatorial Guinea/Malabo	Spanish, pidgin English, Fang, Bubi	Franc CFA
Eritrea/Asmara	Afar, Bilen, Tigre, Kunama, Nara	Nakfa
Estonia/Tallinn	Estonian, Russian, Finnish, English	Kroon
Ethiopia/Addis Ababa	Amharic, English, Tigrigna, Orominga	Birr
Fiji/Suva	Fijian, English, Hindustani	Fiji dollar
Finland/Helsinki	Finnish, Swedish, Lapp, Russian	Euro
France/Paris	French	Euro

Countries of the World, continued . . .

COUNTRY/CAPITAL	MAIN LANGUAGES	CURRENCY
Gabon/Libreville	French, Myene	Franc CFA
Gambia/Banjul	English	Dalasi
Georgia/Tbilisi	Georgian, Russian	Lari
Germany/Berlin	German	Euro
Ghana/Accra	English	Cedi
Greece/Athens	Greek	Drachma
Grenada/St. George's	English, French *patois*	East Caribbean dollar
Guatemala/Guatemala City	Spanish, Indian languages	Quetzal
Guinea/Conakry	French, African languages	Francs
Guinea-Bissau/Bissau	Portuguese, Criolo	Guinea-Bissau peso
Guyana/Georgetown	English, Amerindian languages	Guyana dollar
Haiti/Port-au-Prince	Creole, French	Gourde
Honduras/Tegucigalpa	Spanish, English	Lempira
Hungary/Budapest	Hungarian	Forint
Iceland/Reykjavik	Icelandic	Icelandic krona
India/New Delhi	Hindi, English	Rupee
Indonesia/Jakarta	Bahasa Indonesian, Dutch, English	Rupiah
Iran/Tehran	Persian, Asari, Kurdish, Arabic	Rial
Iraq/Baghdad	Arabic, Kurdish	Iraqi dinar
Ireland/Dublin	English, Irish	Euro
Israel/Jerusalem	Hebrew, Arabic, English	Shekel
Italy/Rome	Italian	Euro
Ivory Coast/Yamoussoukro	French, African languages	Franc CFA
Jamaica/Kingston	English, Jamaican, Creole	Jamaican dollar
Japan/Tokyo	Japanese	Yen
Jordan/Amman	Arabic, English	Jordanian dinar
Kazakhstan/Astana	Kazak, Russian	Tenge
Kenya/Nairobi	English, Swahili	Kenyan shilling
Kiribati/Tarawa	English, Gilbertese	Australian dollar
Korea, North/Pyongyang	Korean	Won
Korea, South/Seoul	Korean, English	Won
Kuwait/Kuwait	Arabic, English	Kuwaiti dinar
Kyrgyzstan/Bishkek	Kyrgyz, Russian	Som
Laos/Vientiane	Lao, French, English	Kip

COUNTRY/CAPITAL	MAIN LANGUAGES	CURRENCY
Latvia/Riga	Latvian	Lats
Lebanon/Beirut	Arabic, French, English	Lebanese pound
Lesotho/Maseru	Sesotho, English, Zulu, Xhosa	Loti
Liberia/Monrovia	English	Liberian dollar
Libya/Tripoli	Arabic, Italian, English	Libyan dinar
Liechtenstein/Vaduz	German, Alemannic dialect	Swiss franc
Lithuania/Vilnius	Lithuanian, Polish, Russian	Litas
Luxembourg/Luxembourg	Luxembourgisch, German, French	Euro
Macedonia/Skopje	Macedonian, Albanian, Turkish	Denar
Madagascar/Antananarivo	French, Malagasy	Malagasy franc
Malawi/Lilongwe	English, Chichewa	Kwacha
Malaysia/Kuala Lumpur	Malay, English, Chinese, Tamil	Ringgit
Maldives/Male	Dhivehi, Arabic, Hindi, English	Maldivian rufiyaa
Mali/Bamako	French, African languages	Franc CFA
Malta/Valletta	Maltese, English	Maltese lira
Marshall Islands/Majuro	English	U.S. dollar
Mauritania/Nouakchott	Arabic, French	Ouguiya
Mauritius/Port Louis	English, French	Rupee
Mexico/Mexico City	Spanish, Indian Languages	Peso
Micronesia/Palikir	English	U.S. dollar
Moldova/Chişnău	Moldovan, Russian	Moldovan leu
Monaco/Monaco	French, English, Italian, Monegasque	French franc
Mongolia/Ulaanbaatar	Mongolian, Turkic, Russian, Chinese	Tugrik
Morocco/Rabat	Arabic, Berber, French, Spanish	Dirham
Mozambique/Maputo	Portuguese, Bantu	Metical
Myanmar/Rangoon	Burmese	Kyat
Namibia/Windhoek	Afrikaans, German, English	Namibian dollar
Nauru/Yaren District	Nauruan, English	Australian dollar
Nepal/Kathmandu	Napali, Newari, Bhutia	Napalese rupee
Netherlands/Amsterdam	Dutch, Frisian	Euro
New Zealand/Wellington	English, Maori	New Zealand dollar
Nicaragua/Managua	Spanish	Córdoba
Niger/Niamey	French, Hausa, Songhai, Arabic	Franc CFA
Nigeria/Abuja	English, Hausa, Yoruba, Ib	Naira
Norway/Oslo	Norwegian	Krone

Countries of the World, continued . . .

COUNTRY/CAPITAL	MAIN LANGUAGES	CURRENCY
Oman/Muscat	Arabic, English	Rial
Pakistan/Islamabad	Punjabi, Sindhi, Pashtu, English	Rupee
Palau/Koror	Palauan, English	U.S. dollar
Panama/Panama City	Spanish, English	Balboa
Papua New Guinea/Port Moresby	English, Tok Pisin	Kina
Paraguay/Asunción	Spanish, Guarani	Guarani
Peru/Lima	Spanish, Quechua, Aymara	Nuevo sol
Philippines/Manila	Philipino, English	Peso
Poland/Warsaw	Polish	Zloty
Portugal/Lisbon	Portuguese	Euro
Qatar/Doha	Arabic, English	Riyal
Romania/Bucharest	Romanian, Hungarian, German	Leu
Russia/Moscow	Russian	Ruble
Rwanda/Kigali	Kinyarwanda, French, English	Franc
Saint Kitts-Nevis/Basseterre	English	East Caribbean dollar
Saint Lucia/Castries	English, French *patois*	East Caribbean dollar
St.Vincent & the Grenadines/Kingstown	English, French *patois*	East Caribbean dollar
Samoa/Apia	Samoan, English	Tala
San Marino/San Marino	Italian	Lira
São Tomé & Príncipe/São Tomé	Portuguese	Dobra
Saudi Arabia/Riyadh	Arabic, English	Riyal
Senegal/Dakar	French, Wolof, Serer	Franc CFA
Serbia and Montenegro/Belgrade	Serbian	New dinar
Seychelles/Victoria	English, French	Rupee
Sierra Leone/Freetown	English, Krio, Mende, Temne	Leone
Singapore/Singapore	Chinese, Malay, Tamil, English	Singapore dollar
Slovakia/Bratislava	Slovak, Hungarian	Koruna
Slovenia/Ljubljana	Slovenian, Serbo-Croatian	Tolar
Solomon Islands/Honiara	Solomon pidgin, English	Solomon Islands dollar
Somalia/Mogadishu	Somali, Arabic, Italian, English	Somalia shilling
South Africa/Pretoria	English, Afrikaans, Zulu, Xhosa	Rand
Spain/Madrid	Spanish, Catalan, Galician, Basque	Euro
Sri Lanka/Colombo	Sinhala, Tamil, English	Sri Lanka rupee
Sudan/Khartoum	Arabic, English	Sudanese pound

COUNTRY/CAPITAL	MAIN LANGUAGES	CURRENCY
Suriname/Paramaribo	Dutch, English, Surinamese	Guilder
Swaziland/Mbabane	English, Swazi	Lilangeni
Sweden/Stockholm	Swedish	Krona
Switzerland/Bern	German, French, Italian, Romansch	Swiss franc
Syria/Damascus	Arabic, French, English	Syrian pound
Taiwan/Taipei	Mandarin Chinese	New Taiwan dollar
Tajikistan/Dushanbe	Tajik	Tajik ruble
Tanzania/Dar es Salaam	Swahili, English	Tanzanian shilling
Thailand/Bangkok	Thai, Chinese, English	Baht
Togo/Lomé	French, Ewé, Mina, Kabye	Franc CFA
Tonga/Nuku'alofa	Tongan, English	Pa'anga
Trinidad and Tobago/Port of Spain	English, Hindi, French, Spanish	Trinidad & Tobago dollar
Tunisia/Tunis	Arabic, French	Tunisian dinar
Turkey/Ankara	Turkish	Turkish lira
Turkmenistan/Ashgabat	Turkmen, Russian, Uzbek	Manat
Tuvalu/Funafuti	Tuvaluan, English	Tuvaluan dollar
Uganda/Kampala	English, Luganda, Swahili, Ateso	Ugandan shilling
Ukraine/Kyiv (Kiev)	Ukrainian	Hryvnia
United Arab Emirates/Abu Dhabi	Arabic, English	U.A.E. dirham
United Kingdom/London	English, Welsh, Scots Gaelic	Pound sterling
United States of America/Washington, D.C.	English	U.S. dollar
Uruguay/Montevideo	Spanish	Peso
Uzbekistan/Tashkent	Uzbek, Russian, Tajik	Uzbekistani som
Vanuatu/Port Vila	English, French, Bislama	Vatu
Vatican City/Vatican City	Italian, Latin	Lira
Venezuela/Caracas	Spanish	Bolivar
Vietnam/Hanoi	Vietnamese, French, English, Chinese	Dong
Yemen/Sanaa	Arabic	Rial
Yugoslavia/Belgrade	Serbian, Albanian	Yugoslav new dinar
Zambia/Lusaka	English	Kwacha
Zimbabwe/Harare	English, Shona, Ndebele	Zimbabwe dollar

What are the world's biggest and smallest countries in terms of their land areas?

Answer: The biggest is still Russia, even after the breakup of the Soviet Union.
The smallest is Vatican City, which is just over 44 hectares (100 acres).

Ancient Gods

People in many cultures created stories about supreme beings to explain the events in their lives. This list gives the names of some of those gods and goddesses. Deities from Greece, Egypt, Rome, and Scandinavian countries often changed roles and names, so you will sometimes see different spellings and responsibilities for many of them.

RESPONSIBILITY	GREEK	EGYPTIAN	NORSE	ROMAN
Supreme god	Zeus	Ammon	Odin	Jupiter
Marriage, fertility	Hera	Isis	Frigg	Juno
Thunder, lightning	Zeus	none	Thor	Jupiter
Water, sea	Poseidon	Sebek	Njørd	Neptune
Sun, sky	Helios	Ra, Horus	Sol	Apollo
Moon	Artemis	Khonsu	Moon	Diana
Fire	Hephaestus	none	Loki	Vulcan
Wisdom	Athena	Thoth	Mimir	Minerva
Love, beauty	Aphrodite	Hathor	Balder	Venus
Earth, agriculture	Demeter	Geb	Jørd	Ceres
War, destruction	Ares	Seth	Tyr	Mars
Wine, fertility	Dionysus	Min	Freya	Bacchus
Underworld	Hades	Osiris	Hel	Pluto
Messenger	Hermes	none	none	Mercury
Peace	Irene	Ma'at	Frey	Pax

The ancient Egyptians believed that their pharaohs were both people and gods. While ruling, the pharaoh was Ra, and when he died he was Osiris. Anubis, the god with the head of a jackal, gave the practice of embalming and creating mummies to the Egyptians.

World Religions

Many religious groups do not keep accurate or up-to-date records, so the numbers of believers reported changes all the time. Looking at percentages is another way to discover what people believe. The percentages on this list are based on a world population of 6,250,000,000.

RELIGIOUS GROUP	NUMBER OF BELIEVERS	(PERCENTAGE)
Baha'is	7,107,000	*
Buddhists	359,981,000	6%
Christians	2,100,000,000	34%
Orthodox	209,000,000	3%
Protestants	421,953,000	7%
Roman Catholics	1,100,000,000	18%
Others	370,000,000	6%
Hindus	900,000,000	15%
Jains	4,218,000	*
Jews	15,000,000	*
Muslims	1,300,000,000	21%
Shintoists	4,000,000	*
Sikhs	23,400,000	*
Spiritists	14,000,000	*
Zoroastrians	1,500,000	*

* Less than 1 percent.

Nonreligious people (those who do not follow a faith) total about 768 million (12%).
Atheists, who deny the existence of a god, have worldwide numbers of 150 million (2%).

Forms of Government

When a group of people live together, they organize themselves using a government. The type of government depends on the will of the people, or the military force of a leader. Canada is a constitutional monarchy. This means that although the Monarch is our Head of State, his or her powers are limited by our Constitution. Over the years Canada's elected representatives and appointed officials have taken over the reins of the decision-making process, and the role of our monarch has become more symbolic.

Anarchy	No organized rule, confusion
Autocracy	One person governs with unlimited power
Communism	One-party system, state controls economy
Democracy	Government ruled by the people, usually the majority
Direct democracy	All people make their laws and vote on them
Representative democracy	People elect representatives to make the laws
Dictatorship	Rule by one person, often through military force
Matriarchy	Rule by a female or group of females
Military junta	Takeover and rule of government by military forces
Monarchy	Rule by a king or queen
Absolute monarchy	Ruler has unlimited power
Constitutional monarchy	Ruler's power is limited by the constitution
Parliamentary monarchy	Ruler is usually a symbol and has little power
Oligarchy	Government ruled by a few powerful people
Plutocracy	Government ruled by wealthy people
Republic	Rule by a chief of state, citizens elect officials
Socialism	Rule by shared ownership of government and goods
Theocracy	Rule by organized religion or religious leaders
Totalitarianism	Rule of the people by the state

PsSST

Humans are not the only ones who organize their lives with a system of government. Animals sometimes choose a leader to head their group. For example, canines will choose an "alpha dog" to lead their pack.

Biggest Cities

Cities in the Canada list are ranked according to the total population of the greater urban area around the main city. In the world list, cities are ranked according to the population of the city and its suburbs.

CANADA		WORLD	
CITY	POP. IN MILLIONS	CITY	POP. IN MILLIONS
Toronto, ON	4.7	Tokyo, Japan	31.2
Montreal, QC	3.3	Mexico City, Mexico	21.5
Vancouver, BC	1.8	São Paulo, Brazil	19.9
Ottawa, ON	1.0	New York, U.S.	18.0
Edmonton, AB	.8	Mumbai (Bombay), India	17.3
Calgary, AB	.8	Los Angeles, U.S.	16.7
Quebec, QC	.7	Kolkata (Calcutta), India	14.3
Winnipeg, MB	.6	Shanghai, China	13.9
Hamilton, ON	.6	Lagos, Nigeria	13.4
London, ON	.4	Buenos Aires, Argentina	13.2

PsSST

It is estimated that the New York City area will fall to eighth on the world list by the year 2015, pushed aside by Lagos, Nigeria; Dhaka, Bangladesh; and Karachi, Pakistan.

Canadian Government Agencies
Alphabet Soup

On the menu for today — Canadian Alphabet Soup! The federal government seems to have an endless supply of agencies and departments. Many go by their initials. You'll recognize some, but others might be a bit obscure.

ACOA	Atlantic Canada Opportunities Agency
AECL	Atomic Energy of Canada Limited
CBSA	Canada Border Services Agency
CCRA	Canada Customs and Revenue Agency
CHN	Canadian Health Network
CMHC	Canada Mortgage and Housing Corporation
CRA	Canada Revenue Agency
CBC	Canadian Broadcasting Corporation
CIDA	Canadian International Development Agency
CRTC	Canadian Radio-television and Telecommunications Commission
CSC	Correctional Service Canada
CSIS	Canadian Security and Intelligence Services
DND	Department of National Defence
FAC	Foreign Affairs Canada
NFB	National Film Board
NSERC	Natural Sciences and Engineering Research Council
RCMP	Royal Canadian Mounted Police
VAC	Veterans' Affairs Canada

See if you know what these initials stand for: EI, CPP, NAFTA, and SIN.

Answers: EI—employment insurance; CPP—Canada Pension Plan; NAFTA—North American Free Trade Agreement; SIN—social insurance number

The Canadian Government

Queen Elizabeth II is Canada's head of state. The governor general is her representative in Canada. The prime minister is the head of the government. The federal or national government is divided into three branches— the executive branch, the legislative branch, and the judicial branch. Here are some of the offices in each of these branches.

EXECUTIVE BRANCH

Governor General
(representing the Queen)

Prime Minister

Cabinet

Cabinet Ministers such as:

Minister of Transport

Minister of Finance

Minister of Intergovernmental Affairs

Minister of the Environment

Minister of Foreign Affairs

Minister of Indian Affairs and Northern Development

Minister of International Trade

Minister of Agriculture and Agri-Food

Minister of National Defence

Minister of Fisheries and Oceans

Minister of Justice

Minister of Citizenship and Immigration

Minister of Health

Minister of Industry

LEGISLATIVE BRANCH

House of Commons (elected)

Government Members of Parliament

Opposition Members of Parliament

Senate

Senators (appointed)

JUDICIAL BRANCH

Supreme Court of Canada (nine judges)

Federal Court of Canada

Provincial courts

Tax Court of Canada

Courts Martial

In Canada, no elected official above the rank of mayor has a specific term of office.

Multicultural Canada

Canada's 2001 census reported that the country's population was 30,007,094. About 5.4 million of those people were immigrants. Here are the top ten countries where most recent immigrants—arriving from 1991 to 2001—were born.

COUNTRY OF BIRTH	% OF RECENT IMMIGRANTS
People's Republic of China	10.8
India	8.5
Philippines	6.7
Hong Kong	6.5
Sri Lanka	3.4
Pakistan	3.2
Taiwan	2.9
United States	2.8
Iran	2.6
Poland	2.4

Sixty-one per cent of immigrants arriving between 1991 and 2001 most often spoke a language other than English or French at home. Here's a list of the top twelve home languages spoken in Canada, according to the 2001 census.

English	21,863,015	Spanish	268,465
French	7,214,280	German	220,685
Chinese (n.o.s.)*	392,950	Arabic	209,240
Italian	371,200	Portuguese	187,475
Cantonese	345,730	Tagalog	185,420
Punjabi	280,535	Polish	163,745

* not otherwise specified

Canada conducts a census once every five years. The 1971 census revealed that the top language spoken at home (other than English or French) was Italian (425,230), followed by German, Ukrainian, Greek, and Chinese (77,890).

United Nations Organizations

Start throwing letters around and sooner or later you will end up with one of the many organizations sponsored by the United Nations. Here is a partial listing of those organizations, which can can be found all around the globe, working hard to make life better for millions of people.

IAEA	International Atomic Energy Agency
IBRD	International Bank for Reconstruction and Development (World Bank)
ICAO	International Civil Aviation Organization
ICC	International Computing Centre
ICJ	International Court of Justice
ICS	International Centre for Science and High Technology
IFAD	International Fund for Agricultural Development
ILI	International Law Institute
IMF	International Monetary Fund
ODCCP	Office for Drug Control and Crime Prevention
OOSA	Office for Outer Space Affairs
UNESCO	United Nations Educational, Scientific, and Cultural Organization
UNEP	United Nations Environment Program
UNICEF	United Nations Children's Fund
UNIS	United Nations International School
UNU	United Nations University
POPIN	United Nations Population Information Network
WHO	World Health Organization
WFP	World Food Program
WMO	World Meteorological Organization

The United Nations employs more than 61,000 people around the world. Its headquarters is in New York City. The leader of the U.N. is called the Secretary-General.

Seven Wonders of the
Ancient World

Scholars in the Middle Ages created a famous list of Seven Wonders of the Ancient World that existed between 3,000 B.C. and A.D. 476. The list was based on structures known to the ancient Greek world.

WONDER/LOCATION	DATE BUILT
Great Pyramid Giza, Egypt	2613–2494 B.C.
Hanging Gardens of Babylon Babylon (near today's Baghdad, Iraq)	604–564 B.C.
Temple of Artemis Ephesus (now Selcuk, Turkey)	550 B.C.
Statue of Zeus Olympia, Greece	435 B.C.
Mausoleum at Halicarnassus Halicarnassus (now Bodrum, Turkey)	350 B.C.
Colossus of Rhodes Rhodes, Greece	282 B.C.
Lighthouse of Alexandria Island of Pharos (now Alexandria, Egypt)	283–246 B.C.

The first of the Seven Wonders of the Ancient World to be built was the Great Pyramid in Giza, Egypt. The Great Pyramid served as Pharaoh Khufu's tomb, and is the only one of the Seven Ancient Wonders still in existence.

Wonders of the
Modern World

Unlike the Seven Wonders of the Ancient World, the wonders of the modern world have never been officially listed. No one can agree on just seven! Here is a list of the human-made structures that would top many experts' lists.

WONDER/LOCATION

Abu Simbel Temple/Egypt
Angkor Wat/Cambodia
Aswan High Dam/Egypt
Aztec Temple in Tenochtitlán/Mexico
Banaue Rice Terraces/Philippines
Big Ben/England
Borobudur Temple/Indonesia
Canadian National Railway/Canada
Channel Tunnel/England–France
CN Tower/Canada
Colosseum/Italy
Dneproges Dam/Russia
Eiffel Tower/France
Empire State Building/U.S.
Gateway Arch/U.S.
Great Wall of China/China
Great Sphinx/Egypt
Golden Gate Bridge/U.S.

WONDER/LOCATION

Hoover Dam/U.S.
Itaipu Dam/Brazil–Paraguay
Leaning Tower of Pisa/Italy
Machu Picchu/Peru
Mayan Temples of Tikal/Guatemala
Moai Statues on Easter Island/Chile
Mont-Saint-Michel/France
Mount Rushmore/U.S.
Panama Canal/Panama
Parthenon/Greece
Persepolis Throne Hall/Iran
Petronas Towers/Malaysia
Shwedaung Pagoda/Myanmar
Statue of Liberty/U.S.
Stonehenge/England
Suez Canal/Egypt
Sydney Opera House/Australia
Taj Mahal/India

Considered by many to be the most beautiful building in the world, the Taj Mahal in Agra, India, is often mistaken for a palace. Emperor Shah Jahan actually had the structure built in 1650 as a tomb for his wife, Mumtaz Mahal.

Victoria Cross

The Victoria Cross was established in 1856 to honour acts of bravery in the armed forces of the British Commonwealth. From that year until 1993, 94 Canadians were awarded this honour. The first Canadian winner was Lt. Alexander Dunn, for actions during the Crimean War. After changing to a different award for a time, a special Canadian Victoria Cross was introduced in 1993, although no one has won it yet. Listed here are the Canadians who won the Victoria Cross most recently, during World War II.

Ian Bazallgette
Aubrey Cosens
David Currie
John Foote
Robert Gray
Charles Hoey
David Hornell
John Mahony
Charles Merritt
Andrew Mynarski
John Osborn
Frederick Peters
Ernest "Smokey" Smith
Frederick Tilston
Frederick Topham
Paul Triquet

A neighbourhood in Winnipeg must have raised its sons right. Three Canadian VC winners—Fred Hall, Leo Clarke, and Robert Shankland—all grew up on Pine Street there. It was later renamed "Valour Road."

Cross of Valour

While the Victoria Cross and numerous other decorations honour members of the military, the Cross of Valour is given to Canadians who have shown exceptional courage and selflessness. The Cross has gone to people who rescued others from fires or drowning, during prison riots, and in terrible storms. Sadly, several of the winners lost their lives in these incidents.

WINNER/YEAR OF AWARD

Lewis Stringer/1972

Vaino Partanen/1972

Mary Dohey/1975

Kenneth Bishop/1976

Jean Swedberg/1976

Thomas Hynes/1978

Gaston Langelier/1979

Amédéo Garrammone/1980

Lester Fudge/1981

Harold Miller/1981

WINNER/YEAR OF AWARD

Martin Sceviour/1981

Anna Lang/1982

Robert Teather/1983

René Jalbert/1984

David Cheverie/1987

John MacLean/1992

Douglas Fader/1994

Keith Mitchell/1998

Bryan Pierce/1998

PsSST

David Cheverie, a police constable in PEI, received the Cross of Valour for risking his life to save three children from a burning house. The year before that, Constable Cheverie had been awarded the Star of Courage for saving a man from a house fire.

Makin' the Law!

The Canadian government follows a step-by-step process to make sure that by the time a law is passed, everyone has had a chance to consider it carefully. Here are the steps that Parliament goes through to turn a bill into the law of the land.

STEP 1 • A new bill is usually proposed in Cabinet for introduction to the House of Commons (or Senate if it originates there).

STEP 2 • A Member of Parliament (MP), usually a cabinet minister, introduces the proposed new law or bill. A senator may also introduce a bill. This step is called the first reading. No debate is allowed: the bill is either accepted or rejected.

STEP 3 • The bill is brought back to the House of Commons (or Senate) so that members can have a debate about the proposed new law. This step is called the second reading.

• The bill is then sent to a committee to be further studied and changed (amended), if necessary.

STEP 4 • The committee's report, along with its amendments, is presented to the House of Commons (or Senate).

STEP 5 • During third reading MPs (or senators) review the bill further. Then they vote on the bill and send it on to the Senate (or House of Commons if it originated in the Senate).

STEP 6 • The bill goes through first, second, and third reading in the Senate (or House of Commons). The Senate may make changes to the bill.

STEP 7 • MPs (or senators) vote to accept or reject any changes made by the senators (or MPs).

STEP 8 • The bill in its final form is sent to the governor general (or his or her representative) for final approval, or royal assent. Then it becomes law.

Bills proposed by provincial governments follow the same first, second, and third reading steps through provincial legislatures, but only once because there are no provincial senates. The provinces' lieutenant-governors give royal assent after a bill passes the third reading.

Rights and Freedoms

In 1982, Canada enacted the Charter of Rights and Freedoms, spelling out rights that belonged to all Canadians. It's a long document, so this list just shows the basic parts of the Charter.

Fundamental Freedoms

Freedom of conscience, religion, opinion, thought, and belief. Freedom of the press, peaceful assembly, and association.

Democratic Rights

Right to vote for Members of Parliament and Members of Provincial Parliament; these members must stand for election at least once every five years.

Mobility Rights

Canadian citizens have the right to enter, remain in, and leave Canada. They can also freely move from province to province.

Legal Rights

Right to life, liberty, and security of the person; protection against unreasonable search and seizure and arbitrary detention. Spells out rules for arrests and indictments for crimes. Protects against cruel and unusual punishment. Protects against self-incrimination.

Equality Rights

Everyone is equal before the law. Protects against discrimination because of race, national or ethnic origin, colour, religion, gender, age, or mental or physical disability.

Official Languages

Establishes English and French as the official languages of Canada, and the right to use either in Parliament.

Minority Language Educational Rights

Gives parents the right to have their children educated in the official language of their choice.

Many people contributed to the development of this document in the years leading up to 1982. But who was the prime minister when it was signed into law?

Answer: Pierre Elliott Trudeau

Big Monuments

Canada has many great sites worth visiting. Some are amazing natural wonders, some have historical significance, and some are impressive structures built by humans. If you're ever in the neighbourhood, be sure to check these out:

SITE	STATE
Athabasca Glacier	Banff National Park, AB
Brock Monument	Queenston Heights, ON
Capilano Suspension Bridge	Vancouver, BC
Citadel	Halifax, NS
CN Tower	Toronto, ON
Confederation Bridge	NB and PE
Dinosaur Provincial Park	Alberta Badlands, AB
Fort Henry	Kingston, ON
Fort Walsh Historic Site	Maple Creek, SK
Fortifications of Quebec	Quebec City, QC
Grosse Île Historic Site	Grosse Île, QC
Head-Smashed-In Buffalo Jump	Fort Macleod, AB
International Peace Garden	Boissevain, MB
L'Anse aux Meadows	St. Lunaire-Griquet, NL

and Landmarks

SITE	STATE
Louisbourg Fortress	Louisbourg, NS
Martyrs' Shrine	Midland, ON
Niagara Falls	Niagara Falls, ON
Parliament Hill	Ottawa, ON
Plains of Abraham	Quebec City, QC
Port-Royal	Annapolis Royal, NS
Riel House Historic Park	St-Vital, MB
Signal Hill	St. John's, NL
Rogers Centre (SkyDome)	Toronto, ON
St. Joseph's Oratory	Montreal, QC
Thunderbird Park	Victoria, BC
Tomb of the Unknown Soldier	Ottawa, ON
Uncle Tom's Cabin	Dresden, ON

PsSST Nova Scotia's beautiful **Peggy's Cove**, with its red and white lighthouse overlooking the Atlantic, is one of the most photographed places in Canada. It is also the site of a memorial to Swissair Flight 111, which crashed in the ocean near the cove in 1998.

Great Inventions

Many of the world's most important inventions can't be tied to any one person or date. Among these are paper from China, the wheel from Mesopotamia, and printing from Japan. Other inventions came about because of need. For instance, 33 years after canned food was invented, someone had to invent the can opener. Wonder what took them so long?

INVENTION	INVENTOR	YEAR
Airplane	Orville and Wilbur Wright	1903
Camera, handheld	George Eastman	1888
Canned food	Nicolas Appert	1811
Can opener	Robert Yeates	1844
Chocolate chips	Ruth Wakefield	1930
Computer language (COBOL)	Grace Hopper	1959
Disposable diapers	Marion Donovan	1951
Elevator	Elisha Graves Otis	1854
Game Boy	Nintendo Company	1989
Helicopter	Igor Sikorsky	1939
Ice-cream freezer	Beulah Henry	1912
IMAX movie system	G. Ferguson, R. Kerr, R. Kroiter	1970
Insulin	Sir Frederick Banting	1922
Kevlar fabric	Stephanie Kwolek	1971
Light bulb	Thomas Edison	1879
Peanut butter	George Washington Carver	1890
Radio	Guglielmo Marconi	1895
Snowmobile	Joseph-Armand Bombardier	1922
Telephone	Alexander Graham Bell	1876
Videotape	Alexander M. Pontiatoff	1956
Virtual reality	Ivan Sutherland	1965

Some inventions are claimed by multiple inventors. The inventor of the automobile could be considered to be Karl Benz in 1885, or Henry Ford in 1896. It depends on your definition of automobile.

Kid Inventors

Kids make great inventors (but you probably knew that). They see a need for a better product, or a better way to do something, and find new and unique ways to solve the problem. We use some of these inventions every day. Young inventors also get involved in invention competitions at their schools. Here are a few inventive kids, their ages, and their creations.

INVENTOR, AGE	INVENTION
Alexia Abernathy, 11	No-spill pet feeding bowl
Eric Brunnelle, 12	Remote-control fish feeder
Frank Epperson, 11	Popsicles
Kevin Germino, 15	Biodegradable fishing lure
Suzanna Goodin, 6	Edible pet spoon
Chester Greenwood, 15	Earmuffs
Charles Johnson, 13	Train detecting device
Jeannie Low, 5	Foldaway kiddie stool
Ivy Summer Lumpkin, 9	Lighted address mailbox
Daniel McKay, 13	Glow Glass — lighted drinking glass
Austin Meggett, 12	Baseball glove and bat carrier
Jessica Peach, 12	Adjustable jump-rope belt
Albert Sadacca, 15	Electric Christmas lights
Brian Schreyer, 17	Emergency traffic signal
Rishi Vasudeva, 17	Biodegradable disposable diaper
Rachel Zimmerman, 12	Computer program for language

Jeannie Low, the inventor of the Kiddie Stool, thought of her invention in kindergarten! She wanted to be able to reach the bathroom sink and invented foldaway steps.

Royal Ranks

In Great Britain, dozens of people run around with royal titles. With most of the titles come land, houses, and money. In the old days, these folks were the rulers of the land. Many of these titles are passed down from parent to child, so to get one, you've got to be born into the right family.

MALE TITLE	FEMALE TITLE	ROYAL FACT
King	Queen	*King* is a word from Old English.
Prince	Princess	From the Latin *principus,* or ruler.
Duke	Duchess	From the Latin *dux,* meaning a leader.
Marquess	Marchioness	Sometimes spelled as Marquis.
Earl	Countess	The oldest English title and rank.
Viscount	Viscountess	Male title pronounced "VY-kownt."
Baron	Baroness	Lowest rank, introduced by the Normans.

There are only **27** men in Great Britain with the title of "duke" at any one time. A son of a duke must wait for his father to die before receiving that family title.

After You...

Canadians don't vote specifically for their choice of prime minister. The leader of the political party that wins the most seats in Parliament becomes the prime minister. So, unlike the vice-president in the United States, the deputy prime minister doesn't automatically take over if a prime minister dies or resigns. Instead, leading members of the majority party recommend their choice for interim leader to the governor general, who swears in that person and asks him or her to form a new government. The majority party then holds a national convention to choose a new leader to become the next prime minister. There may not be a clear line of successors to replace a prime minister, but there is an order of precedence that organizers have to keep in mind when planning official events. Here's a list of some Canadian government officials in descending order of ceremonial "importance."

Queen
Governor General
Prime Minister
Chief Supreme Court Justice
Speaker of the Senate
Speaker of the House of Commons
Ambassadors
High Commissioners
Cabinet Ministers
(from longest serving to newest)

Canada's monarch (also the British monarch) has always been at the top of this list, including Victoria (reigned 1837-1901), Edward VII (1901-1910), and George V (1910-1936). The current monarch is Elizabeth II (1952-   ).

Armed Forces
Whom Do I Salute?

These are the ranks, listed from highest to lowest, of members of the Army branch of the Canadian Forces.

General
Lieutenant General
Major General
Brigadier General
Colonel
Lieutenant Colonel
Major
Captain
Lieutenant
Second Lieutenant
Officer Cadet
Chief Warrant Officer
Master Warrant Officer
Warrant Officer
Sergeant
Master Corporal
Private
Private Recruit

In 1968, the Canadian army, navy, and air force were unified to form the Canadian Armed Forces. One dark green dress uniform was introduced for all members. In 1985, however, they reorganized again and now each branch has its own distinctive uniforms.

Superlative Canada

Canada is a big country . . . second largest in the world behind Russia, in fact, in terms of area. But that's not the only superlative you can attach to Canadian places. Here's a partial list of some of the biggest, tallest, longest, and other "most-ests" from coast to coast.

Tallest mountain	**Mt. Logan** (5,959 m)
Longest river	**Mackenzie River** (4,240 km)
Highest waterfall	**Della Falls** (440 m)
Biggest island	**Baffin Island** (507,450 km²)
Largest lake (Canada/U.S.)	**Lake Superior** (82,101 km²)
Largest lake (all in Canada)	**Great Bear Lake** (31,330 km²)
Deepest lake	**Great Slave Lake** (614 m)
Highest town	**Lake Louise, AB** (1,540 m elevation)
Westernmost town	**Beaver Creek, YT**
Easternmost town	**St. John's, NL**
Southernmost town	**Kingsville, ON**
Northernmost town	**Grise Fiord, NU**
Longest road	**Trans-Canada Highway** (7,604 km)

The Trans-Canada Highway is not just the longest road in Canada; it's the longest national highway in the world. It opened officially in 1962 after more than a dozen years of construction.

From Coast to

Canada's ten provinces and three territories have their own official symbols, as well as their own flags. This list includes information about some of these

PROVINCE OR TERRITORY/CAPITAL

Ontario/Toronto

Quebec/Quebec

Nova Scotia/Halifax

New Brunswick/Fredericton

Manitoba/Winnipeg

British Columbia/Victoria

Prince Edward Island/Charlottetown

Saskatchewan/Regina

Alberta/Edmonton

Newfoundland and Labrador/St. John's

Northwest Territories /Yellowknife

Yukon/Whitehorse

Nunavut/Iqaluit

Did you know that red and white are Canada's official colours? Or that Canada has two official animals—the beaver and the Canadian

Coast to Coast

symbols, along with the provincial capitals. The provincial governments voted to choose which official bird, tree, and flower to name for their province.

BIRD	TREE	FLOWER
common loon	white pine	white trillium
snowy owl	yellow birch	blue flag iris
osprey	red spruce	mayflower
black-capped chickadee	balsam fir	purple violet
great grey owl	white spruce	prairie crocus
Stellar's jay	western red cedar	Pacific dogwood
blue jay	red oak	lady's slipper
sharp-tailed grouse	white birch	western red lily
great horned owl	lodgepole pine	wild rose
Atlantic puffin	black spruce	pitcher plant
gyrfalcon	tamarack	mountain avens
common raven	sub-alpine fir	fireweed
rock ptarmigan	none	purple saxifrage

horse—and two official sports? Can you name our sports and Canada's official tree?

Answer: lacrosse and hockey and—surprise, surprise—the maple tree

Real or Folk?

As North America opened up and people began to explore the unknown lands, brave explorers and pioneers became the objects of tales both true and tall. This list includes real-life heroes and storybook legends.

REAL

Johnny Appleseed (1774–1845)
Frontiersman John Chapman planted apple seeds for pioneers

Daniel Boone (1734–1820)
Pioneer and frontiersman who explored the West

Buffalo Bill (1846–1917)
Frontiersman who shot buffaloes for the railroads and had a western show

Kit Carson (1809–1868)
Frontiersman who explored between the Mississippi River and California

Davy Crockett (1786–1836)
Trapper, explorer, frontiersman, soldier, statesman

Laura Secord (1775–1868)
Canadian heroine of the War of 1812

Sir Samuel Steele (1849–1919)
Famous Canadian Mountie and soldier who helped tame the Klondike

Pocahontas (1595–1617)
Native American in early Virginia who may have saved Captain John Smith

Sacagawea (1788–1812)
Native American guide for the Lewis and Clark expedition

FOLK

Johnny Canuck
Patriotic Canadian symbol, similar to Uncle Sam in the U.S.

Paul Bunyan and Babe the Ox
Larger-than-life lumberjack, accompanied by his pet blue ox, Babe

John Henry
African-American railroad worker, pitted himself against machines

Uncle Sam
Patriotic symbol for the United States

Samuel Steele helped keep order among unruly miners during the Yukon's Klondike Gold Rush. When did that rush for riches begin?

Answer: Gold was discovered in 1896 and the rush began the next year

What's the Date?

You've probably heard the saying "Thirty days have September, April, June, and November. All the rest have 31, excepting February, which has 28 (usually)." Most of the people in the world use this calendar, called the "Gregorian" calendar. However, some cultures use other calendars. Some calendars also change from year to year, depending on the moon, so while the months always occur in these orders, they don't always match up with the Gregorian calendar equivalents, as shown here.

GREGORIAN	ISLAMIC	JEWISH	INDIAN NATIONAL
January	Muharram	Shevat	Caitra
February	Safar	Adar	Vaisakha
March	Rabi I	Nisar	Jyaistha
April	Rabi II	Iyar	Asadha
May	Jumada I	Sivan	Sravana
June	Jumada II	Tammuz	Bhadra
July	Rajab	Av	Asvina
August	Shaíban	Elul	Kartika
September	Ramadan	Tishri	Agahayana
October	Shawwal	Cheshvan	Pausa
November	Dhuíl-Qaídah	Kislev	Magha
December	Dhuíl-Hijjah	Tevet	Phalguna

Note: Spellings may differ based on different sources and translations.

Each of these calendars uses a different year. For instance, if it's 2005 in the Gregorian calendar, then here are the years in other calendars: Islamic 1425-1426; Jewish, 5765-5766; Indian National, Saka era 1926-1927.

THE FIFTY STATES

From the first state of Delaware in 1787 to the last states of Alaska and Hawaii in 1959, the United States of America has admitted 50 states to the Union. Each state has its own identity, often reflected in the state's nickname.

STATE	CAPITAL	NICKNAME	YEAR ADMITTED
Alabama	Montgomery	Yellowhammer State	1819
Alaska	Juneau	The Last Frontier	1959
Arizona	Phoenix	Grand Canyon State	1912
Arkansas	Little Rock	Land of Opportunity	1836
California	Sacramento	Golden State	1850
Colorado	Denver	Centennial State	1876
Connecticut	Hartford	Constitution State	1788
Delaware	Dover	Diamond State	1787
Florida	Tallahassee	Sunshine State	1845
Georgia	Atlanta	Peach State	1788
Hawaii	Honolulu	Aloha State	1959
Idaho	Boise	Gem State	1890
Illinois	Springfield	Prairie State	1818
Indiana	Indianapolis	Hoosier State	1816
Iowa	Des Moines	Hawkeye State	1846
Kansas	Topeka	Sunflower State	1861
Kentucky	Frankfort	Bluegrass State	1792
Louisiana	Baton Rouge	Pelican State	1812
Maine	Augusta	Pine Tree State	1820
Maryland	Annapolis	Free State	1788
Massachusetts	Boston	Bay State	1788
Michigan	Lansing	Wolverine State	1837
Minnesota	St. Paul	North Star State	1858
Mississippi	Jackson	Magnolia State	1817
Missouri	Jefferson City	Show Me State	1821

STATE	CAPITAL	NICKNAME	YEAR ADMITTED
Montana	Helena	Treasure State	1889
Nebraska	Lincoln	Cornhusker State	1867
Nevada	Carson City	Silver State	1864
New Hampshire	Concord	Granite State	1788
New Jersey	Trenton	Garden State	1787
New Mexico	Santa Fe	Land of Enchantment	1912
New York	Albany	Empire State	1788
North Carolina	Raleigh	Tar Heel State	1789
North Dakota	Bismarck	Sioux State	1889
Ohio	Columbus	Buckeye State	1803
Oklahoma	Oklahoma City	Sooner State	1907
Oregon	Salem	Beaver State	1859
Pennsylvania	Harrisburg	Keystone State	1787
Rhode Island	Providence	Ocean State	1790
South Carolina	Columbia	Palmetto State	1788
South Dakota	Pierre	Mount Rushmore State	1889
Tennessee	Nashville	Volunteer State	1796
Texas	Austin	Lone Star State	1845
Utah	Salt Lake City	Beehive State	1896
Vermont	Montpelier	Green Mountain State	1791
Virginia	Richmond	The Old Dominion	1788
Washington	Olympia	Evergreen State	1889
West Virginia	Charleston	Mountain State	1863
Wisconsin	Madison	Badger State	1848
Wyoming	Cheyenne	Equality State	1890

Although not one of the 50 states, Washington, D.C. (District of Columbia), is often mentioned with lists of states. George Washington chose the site for U.S. capital in 1790. Congress moved there from Philadelphia in 1800.

My Representatives

In this chapter, you've read a lot about governments. Canada is a constitutional monarchy, a confederation, and a parliamentary democracy, in which we, as Canadians, elect people to represent us in the government. Even though you can't vote yet, you have people who represent you.

<u>My Head of State</u> _____

<u>My Prime Minister</u> _____

<u>My Governor General</u> _____

My Member of
<u>Parliament</u> _____

<u>My Premier</u> _____

My Member of
Provincial Parliament
<u>or Legislative Assembly</u> _____

<u>My Mayor</u> _____

My Student Body
<u>President</u> _____

<u>My Class President</u> _____

<u>Other Representatives</u> _____

_____

_____

_____

There are usually 105 members of the Canadian Senate. As of 2004, there are 308 members of the House of Commons. They each represent a district called a "riding."

CHAPTER THREE

The World and The Weather

It's a big world . . . but you've got plenty of time to see it all. In here, we've got lists of rivers, mountains, oceans, and more. Check out the weather info so you know what to wear!

Hot Enough for You?

Think it's hot in your classroom on a steamy June day with the windows closed? That's nothin'. Here are the highest temperatures ever recorded in each province and territory. What's the hottest temperature ever? See the box below.

CELSIUS	FAHRENHEIT	LOCATION	DATE
45.0°	113°	Midale, SK	July 5, 1937
44.4°	112°	St. Albans, MB	July 11, 1936
44.4°	112°	Lillooet, BC	July 16, 1941
43.3°	110°	Bassano Dam, AB	July 21, 1931
42.2°	108°	Biscotasing, ON	July 20, 1919
41.7°	107°	Northwest River, NL	August 11, 1914
40.0°	104°	Ville Marie, QC	July 6, 1921
39.4°	103°	Nepisiguit Falls, NB	August 18, 1935
39.4°	103°	Fort Smith, NT	July 18, 1941
38.3°	101°	Collegeville, NS	August 19, 1935
36.7°	98°	Charlottetown, PE	August 19, 1935
36.1°	97°	Mayo, YT	June 14, 1969
33.8°	93°	Arviat, NU	July 22, 1973

Hottest temperature ever recorded? That would be in the little town of Al Aziziyah in the African nation of Libya. On September 13, 1922, it was a pleasant 57.7° C (136° F).

Coldest Places in Canada

Looking for a cold place? No problem in Canada, which stretches nearly all the way up to the North Pole. Here is a list of the lowest temperatures recorded in the Great White North.

CELSIUS	FAHRENHEIT	LOCATION	DATE
-63.0°	-81°	Snag, YT	February 3, 1947
-61.1°	-79°	Fort Vermillion, AB	January 11, 1911
-58.9°	-74°	Smith River, BC	January 31, 1947
-58.3°	-73°	Iroquois Falls, ON	January 23, 1935
-57.8°	-72°	Shepherd Bay, NU	February 13, 1973
-57.2°	-71°	Fort Smith, NT	December 26, 1917
-56.7°	-70°	Prince Albert, SK	February 1, 1893
-54.4°	-66°	Doucet, QC	February 5, 1923
-52.8°	-63°	Norway House, MB	January 9, 1899
-51.1°	-60°	Esker 2, NL	February 17, 1973
-47.2°	-53°	Sisson Dam, NB	February 2, 1955
-41.1°	-42°	Upper Stewiacke, NS	January 31, 1920
-37.2°	-35°	Kilmahumaig, PE	January 26, 1884

What was the coldest temperature ever recorded? Try Vostok Base in Antarctica. On July 21, 1983, they recorded a temperature of -89.2° C (-128.6° F). Brrrr!

Highest Mountain Peaks

The world's highest mountain peaks are located in the Himalayan Mountains in Asia. In fact, the 60-plus highest mountain peaks in the world are all found there. This list names the highest peaks on each continent.

MOUNTAIN/COUNTRY	HEIGHT IN METRES	HEIGHT IN FEET
ASIA		
Mt. Everest/Nepal	8,849	29,035
K2/Nepal	8,611	28,250
AFRICA		
Mt. Kilimanjaro/Tanzania	5,895	19,340
Mt. Kenya/Kenya	5,199	17,058
OCEANIA (AUSTRALASIA)		
Mt. Wilhelm/Papua New Guinea	4,509	14,793
Mt. Giluwe/Papua New Guinea	4,367	14,330
ANTARCTICA		
Vinson Massif	4,897	16,066
Mt. Markham	4,350	14,271
EUROPE		
Mt. Elbrus/Russia	5,642	18,510
Mont Blanc/France–Italy	4,810	15,780
NORTH AMERICA		
Mt. McKinley/United States	6,193	20,320
Mt. Logan/Canada	5,959	19,550
SOUTH AMERICA		
Aconcagua/Argentina	6,960	22,834
Ojos del Salado/Argentina	6,880	22,572

Although Mount Everest is the world's highest mountain, you could also give that award to Hawaii's Mauna Kea. If you measure Mauna Kea from the ocean floor (instead of from sea level), it rises 9,753 m (32,000 feet)!

Volcanoes!

Would you want to be a vulcanologist? Vulcanologists study volcanoes from the air, using airplanes and satellites. They also visit volcanoes in person to monitor their scientific equipment and collect data.

VOLCANO	LOCATION	ERUPTED	VEI*
Tambora	Indonesia	1815	7
Krakatau	Indonesia	1883	6
Novarupta	Alaska, U.S.	1912	6
Pinatubo	Philippines	1991	6
Santa Maria	Guatemala	1902	6
Santorini	Greece	1645 B.C.	6
Taupo	New Zealand	186	6
El Chichon	Mexico	1982	5
Mt. St. Helens	Washington, U.S.	1980	5
Tarawera	New Zealand	1886	5
Mt. Vesuvius	Italy	79	5
Galunggung	Indonesia	1982	4
Laki	Iceland	1783	4
Pelée	Martinique	1902	4
Etna	Italy	1669	3

* VEI stands for volcano explosion intensity, a way of measuring eruptions. The higher the number, the more powerful the eruption and more terrible the damage.

The word *volcano* comes from the name of the Roman fire god, Vulcan. There were supposedly a lot of volcanoes on the planet Vulcan in *Star Trek*.

Largest Lakes

Lakes are usually defined as bodies of water completely surrounded by land. Lakes are generally freshwater, but you will find some lakes with salt water in them. Since the Caspian Sea is a saltwater lake, Lake Superior is the world's largest freshwater lake.

LAKE	BORDERING COUNTRIES	KM²	SQ. MI
Caspian Sea	Azerbaijan, Iran, Kazakhstan, Russia, Turkmenistan	371,000	143,244
Lake Superior	Canada, United States	82,103	31,700
Lake Victoria	Kenya, Tanzania, Uganda	69,484	26,828
Lake Huron	Canada, United States	59,570	23,000
Lake Michigan	Canada, United States	57,757	22,300
Aral Sea	Kazakhstan, Uzbekistan	33,670	13,000
Lake Tanganyika	Burundi, Tanzania, Zaire, Zambia	31,986	12,350
Lake Baikal	Russia	31,598	12,200
Great Bear Lake	Canada	31,328	12,095
Lake Nyasa	Malawi, Mozambique, Tanzania	28,878	11,150
Great Slave Lake	Canada	28,567	11,030
Lake Erie	Canada, United States	25,667	9,910
Lake Winnipeg	Canada	24,390	9,417
Lake Ontario	Canada, United States	19,011	7,340

What lake has dropped on this list?
At 63,973 km² (24,700 square miles), the Aral Sea was once the the world's fourth largest lake. However, the lake has changed size dramatically as rivers that feed into it have been diverted, dropping it to sixth place.

Biggest Deserts

The deserts of the world (some of which are listed by continent below) do not all have the same temperatures. A subtropical desert has a hot climate year-round. A cold winter desert has a range of temperatures. A desert area receives less than 25.4 cm (10 inches) of precipitation per year.

DESERT	KM²	SQ. MI
AFRICA		
Sahara Desert	8.5 million	3.3 million
Kalahari Desert	2.6 million	1 million
Namib Desert	207,970	80,300
ASIA		
Gobi Desert	1.3 million	500,000
Chang Tang Desert	800,310	309,000
Rub' al Khali Desert	647,500	250,000
OCEANIA (AUSTRALASIA)		
Great Sandy Desert	388,500	150,000
Great Victoria Desert	323,750	125,000
Gibson Desert	220,150	85,000
NORTH AMERICA		
Chihuahuan Desert	518,000	200,000
Great Basin Desert	492,100	190,000
Sonoran Desert	310,800	120,000
SOUTH AMERICA		
Patagonian Desert	673,400	260,000
Peruvian Desert	253,820	98,000
Atacama Desert	181,300	70,000

Today's spelling tip: Remember, a *desert* is sandy (one *s*), a *dessert* is sweet and sticky (two *s*'s).

What? No Gilligan?

The size of an island can change. Some islands are covered with ice and snow and are hard to measure. Other islands suffer beach erosion and shrink. This list contains the world's 20 largest islands, but be warned that the order may change.

NAME	OCEAN	KM^2	SQ. MI.
Greenland	Atlantic	2.2 million	839,999
New Guinea	Pacific	820,030	316,615
Borneo	Pacific	743,100	286,914
Madagascar	Indian	587,040	226,657
Baffin	Arctic	476,066	183,810
Sumatra	Indian	473,603	182,859
Honshu	Pacific	230,315	88,925
Great Britain	Atlantic	229,883	88,758
Victoria	Arctic	217,291	83,896
Ellesmere	Arctic	196,236	75,767
Sulawesi	Pacific	189,033	72,986
South Island	Pacific	150,461	58,093
Java	Indian	126,884	48,990
North Island	Pacific	114,687	44,281
Cuba	Atlantic	114,524	44,218
Newfoundland	Atlantic	111,390	43,008
Luzon	Pacific	104,687	40,420
Iceland	Atlantic	102,999	39,768
Mindanao	Pacific	94,630	36,537
Ireland	Atlantic	84,426	32,597

Perhaps the largest island ever was called Pangaea. Many geographers believe that the continents began as one huge landmass. As this landmass, called Pangaea, broke apart, the continents and oceans were formed.

How Deep Is the Ocean?

The ocean depths are among our planet's last unexplored areas. Some trenches on ocean bottoms are so deep that unmanned probes must be used to explore and chart them. In those deep places, sea creatures have adapted to live in cold and darkness, and under tremendous pressure. This list shows the deepest trenches and their depths in feet and metres.

NAME	OCEAN	METRES	FEET
Mariana Trench	Pacific	10,923	35,837
Tonga Trench	Pacific	10,800	35,433
Kermadec Trench	Pacific	10,047	32,963
Philippine Trench	Pacific	10,045	32,955
Bonin Trench	Pacific	9,994	32,788
Kuril Trench	Pacific	9,750	31,988
Izu Trench	Pacific	9,695	31,808
New Britain Trench	Pacific	8,940	29,331
Puerto Rico Trench	Atlantic	8,605	28,232
Yap Trench	Pacific	8,527	27,976
Japan Trench	Pacific	8,412	27,599
South Sandwich Trench	Atlantic	8,325	27,313
Peru–Chile Trench	Pacific	8,064	26,457
Palau Trench	Pacific	8,054	26,424
Romanche Gap	Atlantic	7,728	25,354
Aleutian Trench	Pacific	7,679	25,194

Here are the average depths of the world's major oceans, in metres/feet: Arctic, 1,038/3,407; Atlantic, 3,575/11,730; Indian, 3,840/12,598; Pacific, 3,939/12,925.

World Rivers

Rollin', rollin', rollin' in the rivers of the world. Many of the world's first civilizations were formed next to rivers. Now, billions of people depend on the water from rivers to supply irrigation for farming. Without the rivers, farmers wouldn't be able to provide enough food to feed the world.

RIVER/CONTINENT	LENGTH (KM)	(MI.)
Nile/Africa	6,695	4,160
Amazon/S.America	6,437	4,000
Yangtze/Asia	6,373	3,960
Huang Ho/Asia	5,472	3,400
Ob-Irtysh/Asia	5,407	3,360
Amur/Asia	4,410	2,740
Lena/Asia	4,393	2,730
Congo/Africa	4,377	2,720
Mackenzie/N. America	4,249	2,640
Mekong/Asia	4,184	2,600
Niger/Africa	4,168	2,590
Yenisey/Asia	4,088	2,540
Parana/S. America	3,991	2,480
Mississippi/N. America	3,766	2,340
Missouri/N. America	3,734	2,320
Volga/Europe	3,685	2,290
Purus/S. America	3,380	2,100
Madeira/S. America	3,235	2,010
Sao Francisco/S. America	3,203	1,990
Yukon/N. America	3,186	1,980

Although the Amazon River is shorter than the Nile River, the Amazon has a greater flow of water at its mouth, which is the place where it empties into the Atlantic Ocean.

What Time Is It, Sarge?

People in the military do all sorts of things differently from regular folks. One difference is how they tell time. Military units use a 24-hour clock. This list shows what time it is if you're in the Armed Forces.

REGULAR TIME	MILITARY TIME	REGULAR TIME	MILITARY TIME
1 A.M.	0100	1 P.M.	1300
2 A.M.	0200	2 P.M.	1400
3 A.M.	0300	3 P.M.	1500
4 A.M.	0400	4 P.M.	1600
5 A.M.	0500	5 P.M.	1700
6 A.M.	0600	6 P.M.	1800
7 A.M.	0700	7 P.M.	1900
8 A.M.	0800	8 P.M.	2000
9 A.M.	0900	9 P.M.	2100
10 A.M.	1000	10 P.M.	2200
11 A.M.	1100	11 P.M.	2300
12 noon	1200	12 midnight	2400

Times before 10 A.M., such as 6 A.M., are pronounced "oh-six-hundred hours." For times such as 2 P.M., you'd say "14-hundred hours," and times such as 9:30 P.M. as "21-30 hours."

Types of Clouds

Hey, that cloud looks like a cow! And that one over there looks like a giant slice of apple pie! And that one is an altostratus merging with cirrocumulus, providing a backdrop to the low-lying cumulonimbus clouds! Okay, maybe you won't say that last one, but this list will tell you what it means.

TYPE/DESCRIPTION	HEIGHT IN SKY
Cirrus High, wispy cloud made of particles of ice	**6,100–12,200 m** **20,000–40,000 ft.**
Cirrostratus Thin, transparent, sheetlike high clouds	**6,100–12,200 m** **20,000–40,000 ft.**
Cirrocumulus Thin, high lines of clouds with rippled edges	**6,100–12,200 m** **20,000–40,000 ft.**
Altostratus Greyish sheets of clouds	**1,830–6,100 m** **6,000–20,000 ft.**
Altocumulus Heaped fleecy bands of clouds in blue sky	**1,830–6,100 m** **6,000–20,000 ft.**
Stratocumulus Low, dark, heavy clouds	**1,830 m or lower** **6,000 ft. or lower**
Cumulus Puffy white clouds seen in fair weather	**1,830 m or lower** **6,000 ft. or lower**
Stratus Low, grey, sheetlike clouds producing rain	**1,830 m or lower** **6,000 ft. or lower**
Cumulonimbus Towering clouds; may give heavy showers	**Ground–15,240+ m** **Ground–50,000+ ft.**

PsSST

You can tell how far away a thunderstorm is by timing the difference between seeing the lightning flash and hearing a thunderclap. The less the time, the closer the storm.

Rain...or What?

Precipitation is water that falls from the atmosphere to the earth in different forms. The place with the most rainy days is Mount Waialeale, Hawaii, where rain falls an average of 350 days a year. The driest place on Earth is the Atacama Desert in Chile, with precipitation of less than .002 cm (1/1250 inch) during the year. This list explains the different forms of precipitation you may see . . . or feel!

Rain

Water falling in drops at temperatures above freezing

Snow

Ice crystals that form snowflakes and fall when temperature is below freezing

Sleet

Raindrops that freeze in the cold air before hitting the ground

Drizzle

Light rain made of tiny rain droplets

Hail

Frozen rain in upper atmosphere that collects layers of ice before falling.

Freezing Rain

Water that freezes when it lands on surfaces at temperatures below freezing

Dew

Water that condenses (turns from vapour to liquid) on surfaces

Real super soakers: On November 26, 1970, 3.8 cm (1.5 inches) of rain fell in one minute on the Caribbean island of Guadeloupe. The Canadian single-day rainfall record came at Ucluelet, BC, when 48.9 cm (19.3 inches) fell on October 6, 1967.

Rain Forest Facts

To be considered a tropical rain forest, the forest area must be located between the Tropic of Cancer and the Tropic of Capricorn (two bands of latitude around Earth) and annually receive 102 cm (40 inches) or more of rain. Although they originally covered about 12 percent of Earth's surface, tropical rain forests now cover about half that.

LAYERS OF THE RAIN FOREST, FROM THE GROUND UP:

Ground Layer
Lower Layer
Middle Layer
(also called Understory)
Canopy Layer
Emergent Layer

THREE MAIN REGIONS OF TROPICAL RAIN FORESTS:

Central and South America
West and Central Africa
Southeast Asia

FOODS ORIGINATING IN RAIN FORESTS:

Avocado	Coconut	Papaya
Banana	Coffee	Paprika
Black pepper	Cola	Peanut
Brazil nuts	Corn	Pineapple
Cayenne pepper	Eggplant	Rice
Cassava	Fig	Sugar
Cashews	Ginger	Sweet pepper
Cocoa	Guava	Tomato
Cinnamon	Lemon	Vanilla
Cloves	Orange	Winter squash

Tropical rain forests in South America are part of the Amazon Basin forest, and can be found in nine countries. About 40 percent of the world's tropical rain forests are contained in this Amazon Basin region.

Brrrr!

Some Very Snowy Spots

The U.S. Army Corps of Engineers has identified some of the snowiest spots in the world over different periods of time. Some of the snowfalls listed below accumulated in a matter of hours, while others took months.

LOCATION	CM	IN.	DATE/TIME SPAN
Mt. Baker, Washington	28,951	1,140	1998–1999/one season
Thompson Pass, Alaska	2,474	974	1952–1953/one season
Mt. Copeland, BC	2,446	964	1971–1972/one season
Tamarack, California	990	390	Jan. 1911/one month
Mt. Shasta, California	480	189	Feb. 13–19, 1959/one storm
Thompson Pass, Alaska	444	175	Dec. 26–31, 1955/one storm
Montague, New York	322	127	Dec. 24, 2001–Jan. 1, 2002/one storm
Buffalo, New York	205	81	Dec. 24–28, 2001/one storm
Silver Lake, Colorado	193	76	April 14–15, 1921/24 hours
Bessans, France	173	68	April 5–6, 1969/19 hours
Thompson Pass, Alaska	157	62	Dec. 29, 1955/24 hours

The language spoken by the Aleuts, Native Americans in Alaska, at one time included more than 30 different words that described snow in various forms.

Measuring
The Wind

The Beaufort Wind Scale was devised by Sir Francis Beaufort in 1805 to measure just how fast the wind moves. Along with a speed measured in kilometres per hour, the scale lists some clues to look for. When you see a tree uprooted, for instance, it's a 10 on the Beaufort Scale. It's also a good time to get inside!

FORCE	WIND SPEED kph	mph	DESCRIPTION
0	0–2	0–1	Calm; smoke will rise vertically
1	3–5	1–4	Light air; smoke drifts with wind direction
2	6–11	5–7	Light breeze; can feel wind on the face
3	12–19	8–11	Gentle breeze; leaves and twigs move
4	20–29	12–18	Moderate breeze; raises dust, leaves
5	30–39	19–24	Fresh breeze; small trees sway
6	40–50	25–31	Strong breeze; large branches move
7	51–61	32–38	Moderate gale; large trees sway
8	62–74	39–46	Gale; whole trees move
9	75–87	47–54	Strong gale; slight damage to buildings
10	88–102	55–63	Whole gale; trees are uprooted
11	103–118	64–73	Storm; widespread damage
12	119+	74+	Hurricane

The highest wind speed ever recorded was 371 kph (231 mph) in New Hampshire. Not a good day for flying kites . . .

Quake, Rattle, and Roll

If you've ever felt an earthquake, you know how a bowl of Jell-O feels. But how do scientists measure how strong earthquakes are? They use the Richter magnitude scale, developed by Charles Richter in 1935. Using mathematical formulae, seismographs record the vibrations of the quake as they travel through the ground. The resulting numbers (below) tell people how bad the earthquake was. The distances listed are from the epicentre, which is the spot where the earthquake originates.

Magnitude 1-2 Very minor; recorded on local seismographs but not usually felt

Magnitude 3-4 Minor; often felt, but no damage

Magnitude 5 Moderate; felt widely, slight damage near epicentre

Magnitude 6 Strong; damage to poorly built structures within 10 km (6.2 miles)

Magnitude 7 Major; causes serious damage up to 100 km (62 miles)

Magnitude 8 Great; much destruction, loss of life beyond 100 km (62 miles)

Magnitude 9 Rare and huge; major damage beyond 1,000 km (620 miles)

The largest recorded earthquake occurred on May 22, 1960, in Chile, a 9.5 magnitude on the Richter scale. The largest recorded earthquake in Canada happened off the coast of British Columbia on August 22, 1949; it measured 8.1 on the Richter scale.

Geographical Terms

In geography, you can't really read a map or talk the talk without knowing the right words and terms. Here are the words that will make you sound like a real geographer.

Bay
An opening in the coastline where water reaches into the land.

Continent
One of the seven large landmasses on Earth surrounded by water.

Desert
Dry, almost rainless region of land.

Glacier
A large body of ice that slowly moves over the land.

Gulf
An opening in the coastline larger than a bay.

Hill
Land that is higher than the land around it.

Iceberg
Large section of mostly submerged ice, floating in the water.

Island
Land completely surrounded by water.

Lake
Water completely surrounded by land, usually freshwater.

Mountain
A high piece of land, usually with a pointed or rounded top.

Ocean
One of the five large bodies of salt water on Earth.

Peninsula
Land with water on three sides.

Plain
Flatland.

Prairie
Flatland covered with grass.

River
A large stream of water that runs through the land.

Sea
Large body of water partly surrounded by land.

Source
The place where a river begins, usually in the mountains.

Swamp
Land that is soaked with water, also referred to as a marsh.

Tributary
A body of water that flows into a larger body of water.

Valley
Lowland between hills or mountains.

What do you call the place where a river empties into a larger body of water, such as an ocean or bay? Throat, ear, or mouth?

Answer: It's the mouth of the river.

De-coding the Code

Canada's postal codes are made up of six characters—three letters and three numerals. The characters are arranged in two three-character sets: letter-#-letter, #-letter-#. The first of the six characters indicates one of 18 major geographic regions in Canada. Here's the list of those first letters. More populated provinces are assigned more than one letter. For more information about postal codes, see the bottom of page 124.

FIRST CHARACTER	REGION IT IDENTIFIES
A** ***	Newfoundland and Labrador
B** ***	Nova Scotia
C** ***	Prince Edward Island
E** ***	New Brunswick
G** ***	Quebec (East)
H** ***	Quebec (Montreal)
J** ***	Quebec (West)
K** ***	Ontario (East)
L** ***	Ontario (Central)
M** ***	Ontario (Toronto)
N** ***	Ontario (Southwestern)
P** ***	Ontario (Northern)
R** ***	Manitoba
S** ***	Saskatchewan
T** ***	Alberta
V** ***	British Columbia
X** ***	N.W. Territories, Nunavut
Y** ***	Yukon Territory

If the second character is from 1 to 9, that indicates that it's an urban area serviced by carriers or mailboxes. If it's a 0, it's a rural postal code. Why do you think capital Ds, Fs, Is, Os, Qs, and Us aren't used in the code?

Answer: Because they look like other letters and numbers: 0, E, 1, 0, 0, and V

97

National Parks

Under the direction of Parks Canada, a national agency, Canada is building an enormous network of National Parks. These wide open spaces are designed to preserve the many forms of natural beauty and topography of the nation, from the big pine forests of the southeast to the desolate Arctic beauty of the north to the towering mountains of the west. These are the parks through 2005; more are in the planning stages, so stay tuned!

PARK	PROVINCE
Aulavik	NT
Auyuittuq	NU
Banff	AB
Bruce Peninsula	ON
Cape Breton Highlands	NS
Elk Island	AB
Forillon	QC
Fundy	NB
Georgian Bay Islands	ON
Glacier	BC
Grasslands	SK
Gros Morne	NL
Gulf Islands	BC
Gwaii Haanas	BC
Ivvavik	YT
Jasper	AB
Kejimkujik	NS
Kluane	YT
Kootenay	BC
Kouchibouguac	NB

# of Canada

PARK	PROVINCE
La Mauricie	QC
Mingan Archipelago	QC
Mount Revelstoke	BC
Nahanni	NT
Pacific Rim	BC
Point Pelee	ON
Prince Albert	SK
Prince Edward Island	PE
Pukaskwa	ON
Quttinirpaaq	NU
Riding Mountain	MB
Sirmilik	NU
St. Lawrence Islands	ON
Terra Nova	NL
Tuktut Nogait	NT
Ukkusiksalik	NU
Vuntut	YT
Wapusk	MB
Waterton Lakes	AB
Wood Buffalo	AB/NT
Yoho	BC

Wood Buffalo National Park is larger than the entire country of Switzerland!

Longest Tunnels

Tunnels around the world go under bodies of water or through mountains. In some case, a tunnel begins in one country and ends in another. As this list shows, tunnels can go for kilometres. Most of these tunnels are just for trains; car tunnels are marked with an asterisk (*).

TUNNEL/LOCATION	LENGTH (KM)	(MI.)
Seikan/Japan	55.9	33.5
Channel Tunnel/England–France	51.9	31.1
Laerdal*/Norway	25.4	15.2
Simplon (I, II)/Switzerland–Italy	20.5	12.3
Apennine/Italy	19.1	11.5
St. Gotthard*/Switzerland	17.0	10.2
St. Gotthard/Switzerland	15.5	9.3
Lotschberg/Switzerland	15.1	9.1
Mont Cenis/France	14.1	8.5
New Cascade/Washington, U.S.	13.0	7.8
Vosges/France	11.7	7.0
Flathead/Montana	11.7	7.0
Mt. Blanc*/France-Italy	11.7	7.0
Arlberg/Austria	10.5	6.3
Moffat/Colorado, U.S.	10.3	6.2
Shimizu/Japan	10.1	6.1

The Seikan Tunnel was built without using the huge tunnel boring machines used in most places. The soil beneath Japan's Tsugaru Strait was too soft. Miners used blasting and hand tools to do the job.

Longest Bridges

A log over a stream was probably the first bridge. More likely, a tree fell across the span, and people used it as a bridge. There are many types of bridges in use now: suspension, beam, box girder, arch, and truss. The longest bridges, which include all the ones below, are generally suspension bridges.

BRIDGE/LOCATION	LENGTH (M)	(FT.)
Akashi Kaikyo/Japan	1,990	6,529
Izmit Bay/Turkey	1,668	5,472
Storebaelt/Denmark	1,624	5,328
Humber/England	1,410	4,626
Jiangyin Yangtze/China	1,385	4,543
Tsing Ma/Hong Kong	1,377	4,518
Verrazano-Narrows/New York	1,298	4,260
Golden Gate/California	1,280	4,200
High Coast Bridge/Sweden	1,210	3,969
Mackinac/Michigan	1,158	3,800
Minami Bisan-Seto/Japan	1,100	3,609
Second Bosporus/Turkey	1,090	3,576
First Bosporus/Turkey	1,074	3,524
George Washington/New York	1,067	3,500

The Confederation Bridge, which joins PEI and New Brunswick, is the longest bridge in the world that crosses over waters that freeze. Its main span stretches 250 m (820 feet), but its total length is much longer.

Weird Place Names

Do you think you'd take a trip to Crique Ding-Dong, Quebec? Would people believe you if you told them you lived in Vulcan, Alberta? Canada has lots of unusual place names. Places are usually named for people or for their interesting features. Can you guess how these places got their odd names?

Blow Me Down, NL
Blubber Bay, BC
Bummers' Roost, ON
Burnt Flat, BC
Cow Head, NL
Cupids, NL
Elbow, SK
Eyebrow, SK
Flathead, BC
Head-Smashed-In Buffalo Jump, AB
Horsefly, BC
Jerry's Nose, NL

Legal, AB
Malignant Cove, NS
Meat Cove, NS
Moose Factory, ON
Moose Jaw, SK
Pickle Lake, ON
Pokemouche, NB
St. Louis-du-Ha! Ha!, QC
Sissiboo Falls, NS
Snafu Creek, YT
Sucker River, ON
Tickle Cove, NL

One township in Ontario has the distinction of having the longest place name in Canada: Dysart, Dudley, Harcourt, Guilford, Harburn, Bruton, Havelock, Eyre, and Clyde Township.

Unusual Roadside Attractions

Across Canada, there is a variety of things that people have created just to get their towns on lists like this one. Most of these things are just big — really big. Folks figure the bigger something is, the easier it will be to spot from the highway! And if you spot it, they hope you'll stop and visit.

WHAT IS IT?	WHERE IS IT?
Enormous pop can	Portage la Prairie, MB
Flying saucer	Moonbeam, ON
Giant dogs	Beaupré, QC
Giant "loonie"	Echo Bay, ON
Giant lumberjack	Goodsoil, SK
Giant perogy	Glendon, AB
Giant T-Rex	Drumheller, AB
Huge Adirondack chair	Varney, ON
Huge sundial	Lloydminster, AB
Mac the Moose	Moose Jaw, SK
Mountie Moose	Toronto, ON
Ogopogo statue	Kelowna, BC
World's biggest bathtub	Nanaimo, BC
World's largest lobster	Shediac, NB
World's largest beaver	Beaverlodge, AB
World's biggest salmon	Campbellton, NB
World's biggest tomahawk	Cut Knife, SK

Ogopogo is the Canadian version of Scotland's Loch Ness Monster. Many people claim that this big sea serpent lives in Okanagan Lake in British Columbia.

Canada A-Z

The Canadian Geographical Names Data Base is a rich treasure trove of information, constantly updated with new stuff. You can make dozens of lists from the info in the data base, but we pulled together one that can both get you started and wrap things up. Here are the first five place names listed alphabetically . . . followed by the last five names.

PLACE	PROVINCE
Aachikaayusaakaasich Portage	**QC**
Lac Aachikamakuskasich	**QC**
Aadland Lake	**SK**
Lac Aakaupiynanuch	**QC**
Anse (Bay) Aakulujjuk	**QC**
Zygadene Creek	**BC**
Zymagotitz River	**BC**
Zymoetz River	**BC**
Zytaruk Lake	**MB**
Zywina Lake	**ON**

The data base lists place names for dozens of features, from towns and villages to lakes, mountains, and rivers. Two of our favorites from the list? There's a place name given to an area of "low vegetation" in Nova Scotia, called Aalders Lang Meadow. Off the coast of British Columbia sits a glacier, one of several named in the data base. Good luck pronouncing it: Zexwzaxw Glacier.

Unoriginal Cities

There's just one place called Winnipeg. And there's only one Saskatoon and one Edmonton. But there are two Torontos—one in Ontario and another in Prince Edward Island. And there are 16 Mount Pleasants, 15 Lakeviews, and 15 Centrevilles in the country. Here are some more popular place names that show up across the country.

PLACE NAME	# OF CITIES
Pleasant Valley	14
Fairview	13
Rosedale	11
Salem	10
Bellevue	10
Springfield	10
Glenwood	10
Richmond	10
Riverside	10
Westmount	9

Many lake names aren't very original. For instance, there are 203 Long Lakes in Canada, 182 Mud Lakes, 164 Lacs Long, 109 Round Lakes, and 100 Little Lakes. There are also more than 100 Moose Lakes and Otter Lakes.

My World

Geography is all about the study of the world around us. But what about the world around just you? On this page, make a list of these things about your world. You might have to ask your teacher or parent for help, or check out some stuff in the library or on the Internet. But it's all good stuff to know.

My planet _____

My hemisphere _____

My continent _____

My country _____

My province _____

My provincial capital _____

My county/region _____

My city _____

My neighbourhood _____

My street _____

My house/apartment _____

Bonus:

My city's longitude _____

My city's latitude _____

Nearest river _____

Nearest ocean _____

Do you live in Nunavut? If you do, you're in the newest Canadian territory. On April 1, 1999, Nunavut joined the Yukon and the Northwest Territories as an "official" territory of Canada.

CHAPTER FOUR

Numbers

From counting your change at the candy store
to keeping track of the score at recess,
you use numbers dozens of times a day.
This chapter gives you even more ways
to use numbers, including measuring things,
playing games, and even cooking!

Metric vs.

Canada uses the metric system to measure just about everything. In the late 18th century, the metric system was created by French scientists. Most of the world uses this system, except for the United States, which uses the Imperial system. Because the Imperial system still comes up, it's a good thing to know. This list shows how to convert measurements between systems.

FROM	TO	MULTIPLY BY
Inches	Millimetres	25.4
Millimetres	Inches	.039
Inches	Centimetres	2.54
Centimetres	Inches	.393
Feet	Metres	.304
Metres	Feet	3.28
Square feet	Square metres	.092
Square metres	Square feet	10.76
Yards	Metres	.914
Metres	Yards	1.094
Miles	Kilometres	1.609
Kilometres	Miles	.622

Imperial

For your information, the metric system is also called the International System of Units. Its basic length—a metre—was first measured as 1/10,000,000 of the distance between the Equator and the North Pole. Today, one metre is 1/299,792,548 of the distance light travels for one second in a vacuum. Thank goodness we don't have to calculate that every day!

FROM	TO	MULTIPLY BY
Fluid ounces	**Millilitres**	**29.57**
Millilitres	**Fluid ounces**	**.032**
Quarts	**Litres**	**.946**
Litres	**Quarts**	**1.06**
Gallons	**Litres**	**3.785**
Litres	**Gallons**	**.264**
Pounds	**Kilograms**	**.453**
Kilograms	**Pounds**	**2.2**

How long is long? For many years, standard measurements varied from culture to culture. For instance, a cubit is a measurement from the elbow to the fingertip. In ancient Egypt, a cubit was about the equivalent of 52.4 cm (20.6 inches). The foot varied also. A foot in Rome was 29.6 cm (11.66 inches). In old England, the modern equivalent of a foot was 35.3 cm (13.9 inches).

Ways of Counting

Our number system uses Arabic numerals, so called since they were first drawn that way in Arabia in the Middle Ages. Cardinal numbers are the counting numbers, while ordinal numbers give the order of things. Roman numerals were used in ancient Rome and can still be found today in some places, often as a way of stating the year. The year 2003 would be written as MMIII, 2004 as MMIV, and 2005 as MMV.

CARDINAL	CARDINAL	ORDINAL	ORDINAL	ROMAN
One	1	First	1st	I
Two	2	Second	2nd	II
Three	3	Third	3rd	III
Four	4	Fourth	4th	IV
Five	5	Fifth	5th	V
Six	6	Sixth	6th	VI
Seven	7	Seventh	7th	VII
Eight	8	Eighth	8th	VIII
Nine	9	Ninth	9th	IX
Ten	10	Tenth	10th	X
Eleven	11	Eleventh	11th	XI
Twelve	12	Twelfth	12th	XII
Thirteen	13	Thirteenth	13th	XIII
Fourteen	14	Fourteenth	14th	XIV

CARDINAL	CARDINAL	ORDINAL	ORDINAL	ROMAN
Fifteen	15	Fifteenth	15th	XV
Sixteen	16	Sixteenth	16th	XVI
Seventeen	17	Seventeenth	17th	XVII
Eighteen	18	Eighteenth	18th	XVIII
Nineteen	19	Nineteenth	19th	XIX
Twenty	20	Twentieth	20th	XX
Thirty	30	Thirtieth	30th	XXX
Forty	40	Fortieth	40th	XL
Fifty	50	Fiftieth	50th	L
Sixty	60	Sixtieth	60th	LX
Seventy	70	Seventieth	70th	LXX
Eighty	80	Eightieth	80th	LXXX
Ninety	90	Nintieth	90th	XC
One Hundred	100	Hundredth	100th	C
Five Hundred	500	Five Hundredth	500th	D
One Thousand	1,000	One Thousandth	1,000th	M

To write Roman numerals higher than M, you place a bar on top of a letter. A bar on top of the letter multiplies the value by 1,000. So a bar above an M ($\overline{M}$) would mean 1,000,000.

Prime Numbers

A prime number is any number that can be divided only by itself and one, without a remainder. That automatically leaves out the even numbers and any numbers ending in five (with the exceptions of 2 and 5, which are considered prime numbers). Non-prime numbers are called composite numbers. Here is a list of all the prime numbers between 1 and 1,000.

2	3	5	7	11	13	17	19	23	29	31	37
41	43	47	53	59	61	67	71	73	79	83	89
97	101	103	107	109	113	127	131	137	139	149	151
157	163	167	173	179	181	191	193	197	199	211	223
227	229	233	239	241	251	257	263	269	271	277	281
283	293	307	311	313	317	331	337	347	349	353	359
367	373	379	383	389	397	401	409	419	421	431	433
439	443	449	457	461	463	467	479	487	491	499	503
509	521	523	541	547	557	563	569	571	577	587	593
599	601	607	613	617	619	631	641	643	647	653	659
661	673	677	683	691	701	709	719	727	733	739	743
751	757	761	769	773	787	797	809	811	821	823	827
829	839	853	857	859	863	877	881	883	887	907	911
919	929	937	941	947	953	967	971	977	983	991	997

You may be thinking, what's the big deal about prime numbers? Well, the big deal is that many important math problems you'll run into use prime numbers. It's also good to know prime numbers as you continue doing long division. Knowing prime numbers (or how to find them) will make division easier.

Square Roots

When you "square" a number, you don't put a box around it. You multiply it by itself. For example, the square of 6 is 36 (6 x 6). A number's square root is the number you "square" to equal your original number. So, the square root of 9 is 3 (since 3 x 3 = 9). Get it? Square roots can come in handy when solving all sorts of equations. Here is a list of the square roots of numbers from 2 to 25. (The square root of 1 is . . . 1!) As you can see, they're not always simple numbers. These are decimal approximations in some cases.

$\sqrt{2} = 1.414$

$\sqrt{3} = 1.732$

$\sqrt{4} = 2$

$\sqrt{5} = 2.236$

$\sqrt{6} = 2.449$

$\sqrt{7} = 2.645$

$\sqrt{8} = 2.828$

$\sqrt{9} = 3$

$\sqrt{10} = 3.162$

$\sqrt{11} = 3.316$

$\sqrt{12} = 3.464$

$\sqrt{13} = 3.605$

$\sqrt{14} = 3.741$

$\sqrt{15} = 3.872$

$\sqrt{16} = 4$

$\sqrt{17} = 4.123$

$\sqrt{18} = 4.242$

$\sqrt{19} = 4.358$

$\sqrt{20} = 4.472$

$\sqrt{21} = 4.582$

$\sqrt{22} = 4.690$

$\sqrt{23} = 4.795$

$\sqrt{24} = 4.898$

$\sqrt{25} = 5$

Look for more squares of numbers in the times tables on pages 118–119.

Look for this symbol $\sqrt{}$ to tell you when you will need the square root of a number.

Geometric Shapes

A polygon is a flat, two-dimensional shape that has three or more sides. In other words, polygons have length and width but not depth; a square is a polygon, but a cube is not. Here are the names of a wide variety of polygon shapes, named after their number of sides. Check out all the different kinds of triangles!

**NAME/
SIDES OR DESCRIPTION**

Triangle
three sides

Equilateral triangle
has equal sides and angles

Scalene triangle
all three sides have different lengths

Isosceles triangle
two sides of equal length

Right triangle
two sides meet at a 90-degree angle

Quadrilateral
four sides

Trapezoid
four sides with one pair of parallel sides

Rhombus
four equal sides, but without any right angles

Parallelogram
two pairs of parallel sides

Rectangle
parallelogram with four right angles

Square
rectangle with four equal sides and angles

Pentagon
five sides

Hexagon
six sides

Heptagon
seven sides

Octagon
eight sides

Nonagon
nine sides

Decagon
ten sides

A circle, of course, has no sides and is not a polygon. The official definition of a circle is a set of points on a line, all at an equal distance from the centre of the shape.

What's Cooking?

Teaspoons and ounces and cups — oh my! Cooking has its own world of measurements and numbers that can sometimes be a bit confusing. Plus, in some cookbooks from the U.S., you might see Imperial measurements. Below is a handy chart for switching to metric.

3 teaspoons = 1 tablespoon
16 tablespoons = 1 cup
8 tablespoons = $\frac{1}{2}$ cup
4 tablespoons = $\frac{1}{4}$ cup
1 tablespoon = $\frac{1}{16}$ cup
1 cup = 8 fluid ounces
2 cups = 1 pint
2 pints = 1 quart
2 quarts = $\frac{1}{2}$ gallon
4 quarts = 1 gallon
48 teaspoons = 1 cup

Kitchen Switchin': Imperial to Metric

LIQUID		DRY	
1 tsp.	5 ml*	0.35 oz.	1 g
1 tbs.	13 ml	1 oz.	28 g
1 fluid oz.	30 ml	3.4 oz.	100 g
1 cup	237 ml	1 lb.	454 g
1 pint	473 ml	1.10 lb.	500 g
1 quart	.95 l	2.205 lb., 35 oz.	1 kg
1 gallon	3.8 l		
34 fluid oz.	1 l		

* (ml=millilitre, l=litre, tsp.=teaspoon, tbs.=tablespoon, g=grams, oz.=ounces, lb.=pounds, kg=kilograms)

Because many food products are sold around the world, look for both Imperial and metric measurements listed on the labels of the foods you eat.

Ewww! Fractions!

Come on, they're not that bad. Without fractions, how could you have a slice (⅛) of pizza? Without fractions, how could you get quarters for the video game? (That's right — money is fractions.) Of course, fractions are also written as decimal numbers. This chart lists three ways of writing many of the fractions that you might run across.

FRACTIONS	WORDS	DECIMALS	FRACTIONS	WORDS	DECIMALS
$1/2$	one-half	.5	$1/64$	one-sixty-fourth	.0156
$1/3$	one-third	.3333	$2/3$	two-thirds	.6667
$1/4$	one-fourth	.25	$2/5$	two-fifths	.4
$1/5$	one-fifth	.2	$3/4$	three-fourths	.75
$1/6$	one-sixth	.1667	$3/5$	three-fifths	.6
$1/7$	one-seventh	.1429	$3/8$	three-eighths	.375
$1/8$	one-eighth	.125	$3/10$	three-tenths	.3
$1/9$	one-ninth	.1111	$4/5$	four-fifths	.8
$1/10$	one-tenth	.1	$5/6$	five-sixths	.8333
$1/11$	one-eleventh	.09	$5/8$	five-eighths	.625
$1/16$	one-sixteenth	.0625	$7/8$	seven-eighths	.875
$1/25$	one-twenty-fifth	.04	$7/10$	seven-tenths	.7
$1/32$	one-thirty-second	.0313	$9/10$	nine-tenths	.9

PSSST The quick way to find the decimal number for any fraction is to divide the top number by the bottom number. For example, in ⅝, divide 5 by 8 to get .625. Pick a fraction that's not on our list and try it out.

Multiplication Tables

X	0	1	2	3	4	5
1	0	1	2	3	4	5
2	0	2	4	6	8	10
3	0	3	6	9	12	15
4	0	4	8	12	16	20
5	0	5	10	15	20	25
6	0	6	12	18	24	30
7	0	7	14	21	28	35
8	0	8	16	24	32	40
9	0	9	18	27	36	45
10	0	10	20	30	40	50
11	0	11	22	33	44	55
12	0	12	24	36	48	60

You can use this handy-dandy times-table chart to help you memorize the multiplication tables up through the number 12. Here's an example of how to use it: To find the answer to 8x5, locate the 8 on the top horizontal row of numbers. Then move down the column below the 8 to the place where it crosses the horizontal row that starts with 5 (over on the left-hand side of page 118). Where the column for 8 and the row for 5 meet, you'll find your answer: 40.

6	7	8	9	10	11	12
6	7	8	9	10	11	12
12	14	16	18	20	22	24
18	21	24	27	30	33	36
24	28	32	36	40	44	48
30	35	40	45	50	55	60
36	42	48	54	60	66	72
42	49	56	63	70	77	84
48	56	64	72	80	88	96
54	63	72	81	90	99	108
60	70	80	90	100	110	120
66	77	88	99	110	121	132
72	84	96	108	120	132	144

Ahoy, Matey!

When sailing or going anywhere on the water, such as a lake or an ocean (though probably not your bathtub), you should know the terms for measuring distance, speed, and depth. Who knows? This might make a sailor out of you!

Furlong
201.17 m (220 yards)

Cable*
120 fathoms or 219.46 m (720 feet)

* Can be used to measure distance across water or depth of the water.

International Nautical Mile
8.44 cables or 1,852.96 m (6,076 feet)

League
5 km (3.11 miles)

Knot
Measure of speed on water

One knot
1 nautical mile per hour

Sounding
Taking a measurement of the depth of water

Fathom
1.82 m (6 feet); usually used to measure depth

Mark
1.82 m (6 feet); a riverboat term for depth

The pen name of the famous American author Samuel Clemens is a water measurement. "Mark" is 1.82 m (6 feet); "Mark Twain" is twice that, or 3.64 m (12 feet).

Math Symbols

Do you speak more than one language? Of course you do; everyone who does math of any kind uses a special language made up of numbers and symbols. Here are the meanings of the important symbols you can use in "speaking" this international language.

+	add (plus)
—	subtract (minus)
X or **•**	multiply
÷ or **/**	divide
=	equal to
≠	not equal to
>	greater than
<	less than
≥	greater than or equal to
≤	less than or equal to
%	percentage
:	ratio
π	pi*
X²	a number squared, or multiplied by itself
X³	a number cubed, or multiplied by itself and then by itself again
√	square root (see page 113)
$	dollars
¢	cents

*The measurement called pi (pronounced like pie that you eat) is named for the sixteenth letter of the Greek alphabet. Pi is a number used to help measure the circumference (the distance around) of a circle, as well as the circle's area (the space inside). Pi is about 3.1415.

Cool Math Tricks

Math and magic go together in this list of cool math tricks. Try them on your friends and amaze them with your mathematical mind-reading ability. Just be sure that you do your math correctly!

Back to the Beginning

- Pick any number between 1 and 10 and write it down.
- Write down the next four consecutive numbers following your first number.
- Add these five numbers and divide the sum by 5.
- Subtract 2.
- You now have your original number back!

Math Magic for Class

To find out if any number can be evenly divided by:

2 If the number ends in 0, 2, 4, 6, or 8, it is divisible by 2.

3 Add together the digits of the number. If necessary, repeat until you have a one-digit sum. If the sum is evenly divisible by 3, then so is the original number.

4 If the number's last two digits are 00 or they form a two-digit number evenly divisible by 4, the number is divisible by 4.

5 If the number ends in a 0 or 5, it can be evenly divided by 5.

6 For even numbers only, add the digits. If the sum is evenly divisible by 3, the number can be evenly divided by 6.

9 Add together the digits of the number. If necessary, repeat until you have a one-digit sum. If the sum is evenly divisible by 9, the original number is divisible by 9.

10 If the number ends in 0, it can be divided by 10.

Guess Their Age*

- Ask the person to multiply the first number of his/her age by 5.
- Add 3.
- Double this figure.
- Tell the person to add the second number of his/her age to the figure and have them tell you their answer. Deduct 6 and you will have their age!

(* For kids under 10, their age is the first digit of the result.)

Age Over and Over

- Take your age.
- Multiply it by 7.
- Multiply that product by 1,443.
- Your age shows up over and over in the answer.

Always 18

- Select three different numbers between 1 and 9.
- Write the three numbers down next to one another, largest first, forming a three-digit number.
- Reverse the digits, putting the smallest first, and write this number underneath the first number.
- Subtract the lower three-digit number from the upper three-digit number to get a result.
- The sum of the three digits of the result is always 18!

Here's another trick: To easily multiply double-digit numbers by 11, split the digits of the number. Put the sum of those two digits in the middle. The new number is the answer. Example: 24 x 11. Split 2 and 4; add them and put the resulting 6 in the middle: 264.

My Numbers

You're probably just about numbered-out by this point. Don't worry, just one more list and we promise that you'll know all the answers (or at least you should!). Here is a list of the important numbers in your life.

My favourite number _____

My lucky number _____

My age in years _____

My age in months _____
(years x 12 — see page 118!)

My homeroom or classroom number _____

My phone number _____

My school's phone number _____

My postal code _____

The number of teeth I've lost _____

The number of kids at my school _____

The number of friends that I have _____

The number of times I am told to clean my room before I actually do it _____

My highest score ever on a video or computer game _____

The number of goals I've scored or baskets I've got in my favourite sport _____

The postal code reveals where a letter should go. The first letter in the code tells Canada Post the province or territory; the second character points to urban or rural locations; the third helps narrow the location down further. The second part of the code zeroes in on the local area. See page 97 for more.

CHAPTER FIVE

Science

From the stars in the sky to the rocks in the earth and everything in between, science studies the way the universe works. In this chapter, see how science works!

Sciences and Scientists

Scientists are everywhere! A baker uses science to make a cake rise, and science is used every time someone balances the chemicals in a swimming pool. More important, without science there would be no video games, no e-mail, no bizarrely coloured candy, no hair gel or shampoo, and no skateboard wheels. Here is a list of some of the many types of scientists, the name of their sciences, and what they study.

SCIENTIST/SCIENCE	STUDY OF
Aerospace engineer/Aerospace engineering	aircraft and spacecraft
Anthropologist/Anthropology	human origin and development
Archaeologist/Archaeology	past people and cultures
Astronomer/Astronomy	heavenly bodies
Bacteriologist/Bacteriology	bacteria
Biologist/Biology	life and living organisms
Botanist/Botany	plants
Chemist/Chemistry	relationships between substances and matter
Ecologist/Ecology	plants, animals, and the environment
Endocrinologist/Endocrinology	human glands and hormones
Entomologist/Entomology	insects
Environmentalist/Environment	relationships between all living things
Forensic scientist/Forensic science	science involved in solving crimes
Geneticist/Genetics	genes and hereditary characteristics

SCIENTIST/SCIENCE	STUDY OF
Geologist/Geology	Earth's composition, structure, and changes
Mathematician/Mathematics	relationship of numbers
Marine biologist/Marine biology	life in and surrounding water
Mechanical engineer/Mechanics	interaction of forces and objects
Meteorologist/Meteorology	weather
Metallurgist/Metallurgy	metals
Microbiologist/Microbiology	microscopic organisms
Mineralogist/Mineralogy	minerals
Oceanographer/Oceanography	oceans and ocean life
Paleontologist/Paleontology	fossils
Pharmacist/Pharmacology	drugs, their composition, uses, and effects
Psychologist/Psychology	human and animal behaviour
Physicist/Physics	matter and energy
Sociologist/Sociology	human social behaviour
Zoologist/Zoology	animals

Most of the names of these sciences end in "-ology." This is from a Greek word "logos," which means knowledge. The suffix means "the study of."

Planets

Nine planets revolve around our sun: Mercury, Venus, Earth, Mars, Jupiter, Saturn, Uranus, Neptune, and Pluto. To remember all of them in their order, use a sentence like: **My Very Eager Mother Just Served Us Nine Pizzas.** Or, make up your own sentence. This memory device is called a "mnemonic" [ni-MAHN-ik]. A period of revolution is the amount of time, as measured on Earth, that it takes a planet to complete one orbit around the sun.

PLANET	DIAMETER OF PLANET	GRAVITATIONAL PULL	PERIOD OF REVOLUTION
Mercury	4,880 km/3,032 miles	.38	87.97 days
Venus	12,100 km/7,519 miles	.91	224.70 days
Earth	12,756 km/7,926 miles	1	1 year
Mars	6,750 km/4,194 miles	.38	1.88 years
Jupiter	142,806 km/88,736 miles	2.54	11.9 years
Saturn	120,665 km/74,978 miles	.93	29.5 years
Uranus	51,810 km/32,193 miles	.8	84 years
Neptune	49,528 km/30,775 miles	1.2	164.8 years
Pluto	2,290 km/1,423 miles	.1	248.5 years

Figure out how much you weigh on another planet! Multiply your weight by the "gravitational pull" factors. If you weigh 43.9 kg (97 lb) on Earth and want to compare that to your weight on Mars, multiply 97 by .38. You would weigh about 16.7 kg (37 lb)!

Constellations

By looking up at the night sky you can see star patterns that remind people of mythical figures, animals, and objects. These patterns are called constellations. Here is a list of some of the constellations you can see at various times of the year. Check with your science teacher to get a star chart for your home area, and see how many you can spot.

CONSTELLATION	COMMON NAME	CONSTELLATION	COMMON NAME
Andromeda	Chained Princess	Leo	Lion
Aquarius	Water Bearer	Leo Minor	Little Lion
Aries	Ram	Lepus	Hare
Auriga	Charioteer	Libra	Balance/Scales
Cancer	Crab	Lupus	Wolf
Canes Venatici	Hunting Dogs	Monoceros	Unicorn
Canis Major	Great Dog	Orion	Hunter
Canis Minor	Little Dog	Pegasus	Winged Horse
Capricornus	Sea Goat	Phoenix	Phoenix
Cassiopeia	Queen	Pisces	Fishes
Centaurus	Centaur	Pyxis	Compass
Crater	Cup	Sagittarius	Archer
Cygnus	Swan	Scorpius	Scorpion
Gemini	Twins	Serpens	Serpent
Grus	Crane	Taurus	Bull
Hercules	Hercules	Vela	Sails
Lacerta	Lizard	Vulpecula	Fox

Most of the names of constellations come from the shapes that can be drawn using the stars as points in the shape.

Star Light, Star Bright

It is estimated that there are more than 200 billion stars in the universe. The sun, of course, is the closest star to Earth, and it forms the centre of our solar system. This list of the brightest stars, and the constellations in which they can be located, begins with the brightest star seen from Earth; the stars get dimmer as you move down the list. Ask your teachers or check the library for a star chart of your area to help you find these stars and the constellations listed here and on page 129.

STAR NAME	CONSTELLATION	STAR NAME	CONSTELLATION
Sirius	Canis Major	Hadar	Centaurus
Canopus	Carina	Acrux	Crux
Rigel Kentaurus	Centaurus	Altair	Aquila
Arcturus	Boötes	Antares	Scorpius
Vega	Lyra	Aldebaran	Taurus
Capella	Auriga	Spica	Virgo
Rigel	Orion	Pollux	Gemini
Procyon	Canis Minor	Fomalhaut	Piscis Austrinus
Achernar	Eridanus	Deneb	Cygnus
Betelgeuse	Orion	Regulus	Leo

 Our sun is considered a yellow dwarf star and is estimated to have enough fuel to last another five billion years. At the end of its life, our sun will become a white dwarf, as it collapses under its own weight. Don't worry — like we said, that's billions of years away!

Crowded Space

Stars like those listed on page 130 fill the sky above Earth, but those twinkling lights are not alone. This list describes other heavenly bodies and man-made objects that fill our sky.

Asteroids
Bodies of rock and metal that orbit the sun

Comets
Bodies of ice, dirt, and gas that orbit the sun

Galaxies
Groupings of stars in four types: spiral, barred spiral, elliptical, and irregular

Human-made Space Objects
These include rocket parts, satellites, space stations, and probes

Meteors
Meteoroids that fall through Earth's atmosphere, and are visible as a streak of light

Meteorites
Meteors that reach Earth's surface

Meteoroids
Space debris in the solar system

Moons
Satellites, usually of rock and ice, that orbit around planets. Earth has one moon; Saturn has more than 18 major moons, but many smaller ones. New ones are being discovered all the time!

Planets
Nine heavenly bodies that orbit the sun (See page 128 and note below.)

Stars
Huge bodies of burning gasses; types include blue-white, white, yellow, orange, and red

Like a mystery? There may be a tenth planet, beyond Pluto. Called Planet X, it has yet to be discovered, but is thought to exist because of an unexplained pull on Uranus and Neptune. But then, some astronomers now believe that Pluto is not really a planet at all. Stay tuned!

Classification of Living Things

In order to study life on Earth, scientists have divided all living things into five categories called kingdoms. In order to name a specific organism, seven categories are used. However, we just use common names most of the time.

FIVE KINGDOMS

Animalia
animals

Plantae
plants

Fungi
yeast, mushrooms, mildew, mold

Protista
one-celled organisms

Monera
bacteria, blue-green algae

SEVEN CLASSIFICATIONS

Kingdom
Phylum (animals)
Division (plants)
Class
Order
Family
Genus
Species

EXAMPLES OF CLASSIFICATIONS

COMMON NAME	HUMAN	LION	SWEET BAY
KINGDOM	Animalia	Animalia	Plantae
PHYLUM*	Chordata	Chordata	Magnoliophyta
CLASS	Mammalia	Mammalia	Magnoliopsida
ORDER	Primate	Carnivora	Magnoliales
FAMILY	Hominidae	Felidae	Magnoliaceae
GENUS	Homo	Panthera	Magnolia
SPECIES	Homo sapiens	Leo	M. virginiana

* This category is called a "Division" for plants, such as sweet bay in this example.

The classification of organisms is called taxonomy. Not all taxonomists believe that there are only five kingdoms. Some add a sixth kingdom, Archaebacteria — single-celled organisms that create methane gas.

Food Chain

All living beings take part in the food chain. It works something like this: Grass uses photosynthesis to make its own food and grow. A mouse eats the grass. A snake eats the mouse. A hawk eats the snake. The hawk dies and is broken down by bacteria, becoming part of the soil, which helps more grass grow, and bingo, we're back at the beginning. To borrow a popular phrase, it's the "circle of life."

Step 1. PRODUCERS

Autotrophs: Plants that produce their own food.

EXAMPLES: trees, grass, grains

Step 2. CONSUMERS

Heterotrophs: Organisms that cannot produce their own food.

Primary consumers: Animals that eat plants, called herbivores. EXAMPLES: mice, cows, sheep, rabbits

Secondary consumers: Animals that eat primary consumers. They are usually called carnivores — animals that eat meat. EXAMPLES: snakes, frogs, birds of prey

Tertiary* consumers: Animals that eat secondary consumers. They are called omnivores because they eat both plants and animals. EXAMPLES: squirrels, bears, turtles

Step 3. DECOMPOSERS

Bacteria: Organisms that break down dead plants and animals. This provides nutrients for autotrophs and begins the cycle all over again.

* Tertiary means "third."

What about us? Humans can be either primary, secondary, or tertiary consumers. Whether you enjoy hamburgers, avoid meat, or are even a strict vegan, you're a heterotroph, because you can't produce your own food without help.

What Makes a Plant?

What makes a plant? The answer is cells—lots of them! When cells arrange themselves into specialized tissues, they form the different parts of the plant. All plants have all or most of the parts on this list.

Roots

Roots anchor and hold the plant in the ground or water, while absorbing water and minerals.

Stems

Stems support the plant and hold leaves up to the light. Inside stems, xylem tissue transports water and minerals up from the roots, while phloem tissue takes the leaf-produced food throughout the plant.

Leaves

Leaves are the areas of a plant that produce its food. Plants use light energy, water, and carbon dioxide to produce food, releasing oxygen. Green stuff called chlorophyll gathers the energy from the sun.

Seeds

Seeds are the part of the plant that reproduces.

Flowers

Seeds are made in the flowering part of the plants. Flower parts include stamens, anthers, stylem, fruit, and petals.

PSSST

Plants that contain both male and female parts of the reproductive system in one flower are known as perfect flowers.

Inside the Animal Kingdom

The animal kingdom consists of many-celled organisms. They are divided into classes (see page 132). Here are the animal classes, some of the characteristics that animals in each class share, and examples of each class.

INVERTEBRATES
Multicelled organisms without backbones

Annelida
soft, segmented body, two body openings (earthworms, leeches)

Arthropoda
jointed legs, segmented body: arachnids (spiders, ticks); crustaceans (crabs, shrimp); insects (fleas, crickets)

Coelenterata
tentacles, stinger cells, primitive nervous systems (corals, jellyfish, sea anemones)

Echinodermata
tube feet, no head, can regenerate body parts, aquatic (sand dollars, sea urchins, starfish)

Mollusca
soft body, usually a hard shell, head, sense organs, aquatic (clams, octopuses, snails)

Nematoda
smooth outer skin, pointed ends, usually microscopic (nematodes, pinworms)

Platyhelminthes
head, simple nervous system, lives in wet environments (tapeworms, flukes)

Porifera
live in colonies, attach to underwater rocks (sponges)

VERTEBRATES
Animals with backbones

Amphibia
lay eggs, live in water and on land, true legs, gills grow into lungs (frogs, salamanders)

Aves (Birds)
warm-blooded, feathers, wings, bills, lay eggs, most fly (owls, ostriches, robins)

Fish
scales, aquatic, gills, fins, lay eggs (rays, sharks, goldfish)

Mammalia
hair, bear their young live, produce milk, warm-blooded (mice, humans, whales)

Reptilia
lay eggs, scales, lungs, most cold-blooded (crocodiles, alligators, turtles, snakes)

The category of Arthropoda has more than 80 percent of the animals in the world. In other words, insects rule the planet!

Stuff We Grow to Eat

Our bodies can't produce our own food. We have to depend on food-producing plants (and animals) for our nutrition. Lucky for us, growing plants for our food supply is a big business. Farmers plant, cultivate, and harvest the plants that we need to keep ourselves healthy. Here are examples from the four major groups of plant foods.

FRUITS

Apple, blackberry, blueberry, fig, mango, peach, pear, pineapple, strawberry

GRAINS

Alfalfa, barley, millet, oats, rice, rye, wheat

NUTS*

Almond, cashew, filbert, pecan, pistachio, walnut

VEGETABLES

Asparagus, carrot, corn, eggplant, soybean, onion, pea, sweet potato

* Cool fact: Peanuts are not nuts! They're technically considered vegetables.

We eat plants; what about plants that eat meat? The Venus-flytrap plant eats flies, spiders, and slugs. Other meat-eating plants include bladderworts, pitcher plants, and the European butterwort.

Medicines from Plants

Besides providing beauty and food, plants can help cure our aches and pains. We still have many plants to examine for their medicinal properties, and it is important to discover them before they disappear from our planet. This list provides a small sample of the hundreds of ways in which plants help us. **Do not**, however, try any of these remedies unless you have checked with your doctor first.

PLANT	HELPS WITH . . .
Aloe	easing sunburns
Chili pepper	reducing pain
Eucalyptus	killing germs
Garlic	infections
Ginger	digestion
Mint	nausea, indigestion
Pacific yew	fighting cancer
Purple coneflower	resisting infection
Rose	Vitamin C
St. John's wort	nervous system
Willow	headaches, fevers
Wormwood	parasitic worms
Yarrow	nosebleeds

PsSST Found in Asia, the Neem tree (*Azadirachta indica*) can be used in many ways: to get rid of athlete's foot, ringworm, and lice; to treat malaria and fever; to prevent viral diseases; and even as a toothpaste!

A Fossil Time Line

The remains of plants and animals in rocks, or outlines of them, are called fossils. A fossil can be a small part of a leaf, a shark's tooth, an insect, or part of an early human. Fossils give us the history of plants and animals that no longer exist. Here are some key moments in the history of fossils.

1780
First fossils of dinosaur bones found in England.

1811
First ichthyosaur* fossil found in England.

1856
Hominoid (early human) skull fragment fossil found in Germany.

1860
Earliest-known bird fossil found.

1974
Complete skeleton of early human (*Australopithecus afarensis*) found in Ethiopia; named "Lucy."

1976
Footprints of *Australopithecus afarensis* found in Tanzania.

1987
Oldest known fossil dinosaur egg embryo (more than 230 million years old) found.

1991
Body of a 5,000-year-old man, preserved in ice, found in the Italian Alps.

"Lucy's Grandson," *Australopithecus afarensis*, male skull found in Ethiopia.

2002
"Toumai," 7-million-year-old hominoid fossil found in Africa.

2004
Fossils of tiny "Hobbit-sized" humanoids found in a cave in Indonesia.

* A flying dinosaur; found by an explorer named Mary Anning.

Coelacanth (**SEEL-uh-kanth**) fossils have been found that date this fish to 400 million years ago. In 1938, and again in 1998, live coelacanths were caught. This fish, once thought extinct, is known as a "living fossil"!

Earth's Eras

Earth's history is divided into four eras, or very long time periods. We use fossil and geological records to discover in what era various living things existed. Each era is broken up into periods. All numbers below (except the first) are in "millions of years ago."

ERA/PERIOD	MILLIONS OF YEARS AGO	LIVING THINGS
Precambrian Era	**4.5 billion–600 million**	
		one-celled organisms
Paleozoic Era	**600–245**	
Cambrian	600–510	fossil records of hard-shell animals
Ordovician	510–439	animal life in the oceans
Silurian	439–408	first land plants evolve, reefs build up
Devonian	408–360	land plants and amphibians evolve
Carboniferous	360–290	amphibians and reptiles evolve
Permian	290–245	cone-bearing plants and reptiles evolve
Mesozoic Era	**245–65**	
Triassic	245–208	mammals
Jurassic	208–144.2	dinosaurs
Cretaceous	144.2–65	more dinosaurs
Cenozoic Era	**65–today**	
Tertiary	65–1.64	apes and humanoids
Quaternary	1.64–today	finally — people!

Most scientists now agree that a massive meteor that struck Earth near Mexico about 65 million years ago was one of the main reasons dinosaurs suddenly disappeared.

It's Element-ary

We're not talking elementary school here. Science has figured out that all substances on Earth are made of the same basic elements. That is, they are made of substances that cannot be broken down any further. These elements are listed here alphabetically, but they also can be arranged according to their atomic number in the periodic table of the elements.

NAME	SYMBOL	ATOMIC NUMBER	NAME	SYMBOL	ATOMIC NUMBER
Actinium	Ac	89	Erbium	Er	68
Aluminum	Al	13	Europium	Eu	63
Americium	Am	95	Fermium	Fm	100
Antimony	Sb	51	Fluorine	F	9
Argon	Ar	18	Francium	Fr	87
Arsenic	As	33	Gadolinium	Gd	64
Astatine	At	85	Gallium	Ga	31
Barium	Ba	56	Germanium	Ge	32
Berkelium	Bk	97	Gold	Au	79
Beryllium	Be	4	Hafnium	Hf	72
Bismuth	Bi	83	Hassium*	Mt	108
Bohrium*	Bh	107	Helium	He	2
Boron	B	5	Holmium	Ho	67
Bromine	Br	35	Hydrogen	H	1
Cadmium	Cd	48	Indium	In	49
Calcium	Ca	20	Iodine	I	53
Californium	Cf	98	Iridium	Ir	77
Carbon	C	6	Iron	Fe	26
Cerium	Ce	58	Krypton	Kr	36
Cesium	Cs	55	Lanthanum	La	57
Chlorine	Cl	17	Lawrencium	Lr	103
Chromium	Cr	24	Lead	Pb	82
Cobalt	Co	27	Lithium	Li	3
Copper	Cu	29	Lutetium	Lu	71
Curium	Cm	96	Magnesium	Mg	12
Dubnium*	Db	105	Manganese	Mn	25
Dysprosium	Dy	66	Meitnerium*	Mt	109
Einsteinium	Es	99	Mendelevium	Md	101

NAME	SYMBOL	ATOMIC NUMBER	NAME	SYMBOL	ATOMIC NUMBER
Mercury	Hg	80	Selenium	Se	34
Molybdenum	Mo	42	Silicon	Si	14
Neodymium	Nd	60	Silver	Ag	47
Neon	Ne	10	Sodium	Na	11
Neptunium	Np	93	Strontium	Sr	38
Nickel	Ni	28	Sulphur	S	16
Niobium	Nb	41	Tantalum	Ta	73
Nitrogen	N	7	Technetium	Tc	43
Nobelium	No	102	Tellurium	Te	52
Osmium	Os	76	Terbium	Tb	65
Oxygen	O	8	Thallium	Tl	81
Palladium	Pd	46	Thorium	Th	90
Phosphorus	P	15	Thulium	Tm	69
Platinum	Pt	78	Tin	Sn	50
Plutonium	Pu	94	Titanium	Ti	22
Polonium	Po	84	Tungsten	W	74
Potassium	K	19	Ununbium	Uub	112
Praseodymium	Pr	59	Ununhexium	Uuh	116
Promethium	Pm	61	Ununium	Uuu	111
Protactinium	Pa	91	Ununnilium	Uun	110
Radium	Ra	88	Ununoctium	Uuo	118
Radon	Rn	86	Ununquadium	Uuq	114
Rhenium	Re	75	Uranium	U	92
Rhodium	Rh	45	Vanadium	V	23
Rubidium	Rb	37	Xenon	Xe	54
Ruthenium	Ru	44	Ytterbium	Yb	70
Rutherfordium*	Rf	104	Yttrium	Y	39
Samarium	Sm	62	Zinc	Zn	30
Scandium	Sc	21	Zirconium	Zr	40
Seaborgium*	Sg	106			

* You might see these elements called by other names; scientists can't agree on which names to use.

Dmitry Mendeleyev organized the elements into what is called the Periodic Table of the Elements. Forty-five years later, in 1914, Henry G. J. Moseley rearranged the table using the atomic numbers of the elements.

Forms of Energy

Energy can be divided into two categories: potential (energy stored for later use) and kinetic (energy in motion). We cannot create or destroy energy, but the forms of energy can be changed.

Atomic

Fission: splitting of atomic nucleus
EXAMPLE: atomic power plant
Fusion: joining together of two atomic nuclei
EXAMPLE: nuclear bomb

Chemical

Energy produced when converting raw materials.
EXAMPLES: fire, coal, oil, natural gas

Electrical

Energy produced by the flow of electrons through wire lines; turned into heat, light, mechanical energy. EXAMPLES: batteries, generators

Geothermal

Energy produced from heat inside Earth, used to produce electricity.
EXAMPLES: steam, geysers

Heat

Energy produced through the vibration of molecules or atoms.
EXAMPLES: radiator, stove

Hydroelectric

Electric energy produced by water power.
EXAMPLES: waterwheels, dams

Magnetic

Energy produced through moving charged particles.
EXAMPLE: electromagnets

Solar

Energy produced by turning sunlight into energy.
EXAMPLES: solar panels heating water, producing steam

Sound

Energy produced by the vibration of molecules as sound is carried through air.
EXAMPLES: radio, telegraph

Thermodynamics

Energy produced by the transfer of heat into other forms of energy and back.
EXAMPLE: refrigeration

Wind

Energy produced by using wind to turn or revolve propeller turbines.
EXAMPLE: windmills

Most of our energy comes from the sun. Solar energy heats the earth after travelling more than 155 million km (93 million miles). That light travels through space at 299,792 km (1.86 million miles) per second.

Machines

Machines are more than just big, metal things that manufacture cars, clean streets, or make concrete. A machine is any device that makes work easier by using energy to overcome or change the direction of a force, and give a mechanical advantage. Scientists created these categories of machines.

Simple Machines

These basic machines are used to accomplish different types of work. All six machines involve a load and an effort, that is, taking something and moving it in a particular direction.

Inclined plane
Surface raised in an inclined position, a ramp

Lever
Different ways of lifting things, such as crowbars, wheelbarrows, or a lifting arm

Pulley
Rope or chain placed over a wheel or track in a wheel

Screw
An inclined plane twisting around an axis, such as a blender or a ship's propeller

Wheel and axle
Round frame on central rod, such as a bicycle tire or car wheels

Wedge
Two or more sloping surfaces tapering to a thin edge, such as an axe

Complex Machines

These are any combination of simple machines that work together to perform their job. Among the millions of different types of complex machines are:

airplanes, automobiles, cameras, computers, telephones, televisions

Can machines think? Some scientists are working on ways to make computers do more than just what we tell them to. The science of "artificial intelligence" is trying to build computers that can have original thoughts.

Systems of the Human Body

Twenty-four hours, seven days a week, your body systems function, enabling you to move, eat, play video games, and do your homework. Some systems and organs do their jobs without your permission, such as your heart. Other systems wait for your directions, such as muscles that make you walk. Here are the systems that keep your body humming, along with some of their key organs.

Circulatory carries blood throughout the body
PARTS: heart, veins, arteries

Digestive breaks down food into nutrients
PARTS: mouth, stomach, intestines

Excretory removes waste products
PARTS: kidneys, colon

Muscular helps with movement
PARTS: muscles

Nervous controls nerves, the responses of the body
PARTS: brain, spinal cord

Reproductive system used to create offspring
PARTS: ovaries (female); testes (male)

Respiratory takes in carbon dioxide and exchanges it for oxygen PARTS: mouth, nose, lungs

Skeletal provides framework and support
PARTS: 206 bones, cartilage, ligaments

Immune provides protection from disease and infection PARTS: lymph nodes, skin

What's missing here? Your senses. Your ears, eyes, tongue, skin, and nose all do specific jobs, and are also considered part of the nervous system.

Boning Up on Bones

You have 206 bones in your body. Most of them make up your arms, hands, legs, and toes. Check out the number of bones it takes to have working ankles and wrists — no wonder it takes so long for them to heal! Here are the number of bones in various parts of your body. Add 'em up and you'll get 206.

BODY SECTION	NO. OF BONES
Cranium (skull)	**22**
Ears	**6**
Spine	**26**
Ribs	**24**
Sternum (breastbone)	**1**
Throat (hyoid bone)	**1**
Shoulders	**4**
Forearms	**6**
Wrists (carpus)	**26**
Fingers (phalanges)	**28**
Hips	**2**
Legs	**8**
Ankles (tarsus)	**24**
Toes (phalanges)	**28**
TOTAL	**206**

PsSST

Without your hammer, anvil, and stirrups, you couldn't hear someone read out loud. These three bones in the ear are the tiniest bones in your body, but they have a vital function in helping you hear.

Mighty Muscles

You have three types of muscles: heart, smooth, and striped. Of course, the heart muscles are found in your heart. Smooth muscles are found in your organs, such as your stomach. Striped muscles make up your skeletal, or voluntary, muscles. On this list are the muscles that you may have heard about; they're the muscles you use to move around in the world.

Biceps
bends your arm

Brachioradialis
bends your elbow

Deltoid
moves your shoulder

Flexor
moves your hand

Gastrocnemius
used to walk and jump

Gracilis
bends and twists your leg

Pectoralis major
used to breathe and move your shoulders

Quadriceps
straightens your leg

Rectus femoris
moves your thigh

Sartorius
bends your leg

Soleus
used to stand

Tibialis anterior
used to walk

Trapezius
keeps your shoulders straight

Triceps
straightens your arm

Vastus lateralis
extends your knee

Vastus medialis
bends and extends your knee

How many muscles does your face need to help you smile, frown, show surprise, show fear, or display other emotions? A. 10 B. 40 C. 80.

Answer: Forty in all. And that's all the muscles in your face, working together to show whatever emotion you're feeling.

My Gooey Body

Everyone tells you that your body is mostly water, but there are many types of fluid running through and out of your body. Some of these fluids can be quite messy, but they are all necessary to keep you healthy, lubricated, and moving.

Bile
made by the liver, used to break down fats

Blood
transports nutrients and oxygen to the body cells

Chyme
in the stomach, breaks down food into liquid form

Diarrhea
watery solid waste

Gastric juice
stomach fluids, enzymes, and acids

Inner-ear fluid
in the inner ear, used to help keep balance

Lymph
yellow liquid found in the lymphatic system

Mucus
protective fluid of membrane linings, such as those in the nose

Pus
dead bacteria and cells

Rhinorrhea
fluid running from your nose

Saliva
in the mouth, used to begin digestive process

Synovial fluid
lubricates cartilage, movable joints

Tears
produced to wash dust out of eyes

Urine
produced by the kidneys, then eliminated from the body

Vomit
stomach fluid ejected from body through the esophagus and the mouth

Rhinorrhea and mucus come flying out of your nose at more than 100 kph (60 mph) when you sneeze. It's impossible to keep your eyes open when you sneeze — probably to keep rhinorrhea out of your eyes!

First Aid Kit

The Red Cross and local fire departments recommend that every family have a first aid kit somewhere in the home. It's also a good idea to keep a smaller one in the car. You can buy premade kits at a drugstore, or you can create your own. Here are the basic items that the Red Cross suggests that you keep in your home first aid kit. They also recommend that you include a list of emergency phone numbers and a first aid manual.

Adhesive tape
Blanket
Cold pack
Disposable gloves
Elastic wrap
Gauze pads
Gauze rolls (various sizes)
Hand cleaner
Plastic adhesive bandages (various sizes)
Scissors
Tweezers
Small flashlight
Spare batteries
Triangular bandage

* Along with these materials, your parents might want to include medicines such as Aspirin or an antiseptic (germ-killing) ointment.

Emergency experts say that every kid should know how to call for help in an emergency. In most communities, you dial 911 on the phone. Ask your family what the number is in your area. Also, make sure you know your own phone number and address when you call. This will make sure that help gets there fast.

Stuff in Your Mouth

You need your mouth for a lot of stuff. You use it to breathe, chew, whistle, sing, talk, yell, kiss, cough, spit, and vomit. Your mouth and its parts are mighty important, so take good care of yours — you only get one.

Jaw bony structure that supports teeth, helps open and close the mouth, protects soft mouth tissue

Cheeks soft tissue, fleshy sides of mouth

Palate roof of your mouth; two sections — soft and hard

Lips outer folds of the mouth

Teeth bonelike structures in the jaw that help with chewing; hardest substance in the body

Gums tissue that surrounds and holds the teeth

Tongue organ that helps with speaking and digestion process of tasting, chewing, and swallowing

Papillae bumpy surface of the tongue

Taste buds cells on the surface of the tongue used to taste

Taste hairs tiny hairs on top of the taste buds

Tongue nerves three: two for taste, one for movement

Tonsils part of the throat; thought to protect against infections

Saliva fluid in the mouth consisting of enzymes that begin the digestive process

Uvula fleshy knob that hangs from the back of the roof of your mouth

You can make a map of your tongue. Use different foods to find four tastes. Look for the sweet taste at the tip of your tongue, the salty along the sides in the front, the sour along the sides near the rear, and the bitter toward the back of your tongue.

Seeing into Your Eye

Your eyes are among the most amazing structures ever invented — or evolved, or created, or whatever. Eyes actually need many moving, complicated parts to take in light and reveal to our brains just what it says on the chalkboard at the front of class — among other things. Here are all the parts of your eyes.

Blood vessels
carry blood to and from the eye, taking nutrients to cells

Cones
cells that are part of the retina, used to see colours and clear images

Cornea
transparent outside of your eye; covers iris and pupil

Iris
coloured part of the eye that opens and closes, allowing light to enter

Lens
clear part of the eye that focuses the images

Optic nerve
nerve that takes signals from the retina to the brain

Pupil
opening in the iris through which light enters the eye

Retina
lining in the back of the eye, contains cones and rods

Rods
cells that are part of the retina; used to see in dim light

Sclera
outer covering of the eyeball, the "whites" of your eyes

Vitreous humour
clear jellylike fluid contained in the eyeball

You see the world upside down. Seriously: the image your retina transfers to your brain through the optic nerve is the wrong way up. Your retina uses more than 125 million cones and rods to send the image. Your brain interprets and flips the image around so you see the world in a normal position.

Rocks and Minerals

Although we often use the terms "rocks" and "minerals" together, they are different. Minerals (marked with * on this list) consist of one or more elements (see page 140), while rocks consist of one or more minerals. Here are some examples of rocks and minerals you may have run across.

Agate
Aquamarine
Basalt
Borax*
Corundum*
Diamond*
Emerald*
Garnet*
Gold*
Granite
Graphite*
Gypsum*
Limestone

Obsidian
Opal
Platinum*
Pyrite*
Quartz
Ruby*
Sandstone
Shale
Silver*
Sulphur*
Turquoise
Zircon

Rocks are classified by how they were formed. IGNEOUS rocks are formed from magma or lava. Examples: granite, obsidian, pumice. SEDIMENTARY rocks are formed over long periods of time by the buildup of layers of rock fragments, dirt, sand, mud, or clay. Examples: limestone, sandstone, shale. METAMORPHIC rocks are formed from other rocks that have been subjected to heat and pressure. Examples: coal, marble, slate.

To test the hardness of minerals, geologists use Mohs' scale, with a range from 1 to 10 (softest to hardest). Here are examples of all the levels on Mohs' scale: Talc 1; Gypsum 2; Calcite 3; Fluorite 4; Apatite 5; Orthoclase 6; Quartz 7; Topaz 8; Corundum 9; Diamond 10.

Living with Rocks

Believe it or not, we use all kinds of rocks and minerals every day. We write with them (graphite pencils), build our homes with them (gypsum walls), brush our teeth with them (fluoride toothpaste), and even wear them on our bodies (silver and gold jewellery). Some of the other uses might surprise you.

ROCK OR MINERAL/USED IN OR AS . . .

Aluminum   cans, planes, automobiles, sports equipment

Coal   energy source

Copper   wire, brass, bronze, coins, jewellery, cooking utensils

Gold   jewellery, dentistry, medicine, coins, computers, electronics

Graphite   pencils

Gypsum   drywall

Iron   cookware, steel for cars, cans, construction, appliances

Lead   batteries, radiation shielding

Limestone   cement, antacid medicine

Marble   construction, household items

Salt   food, food preservation, to melt ice, water treatment

Silica   food products, computer chips, glass, ceramics

Silver   photography, jewellery, coins, mirrors, dentistry

Slate   roofs, gardens, billiard tables

Sulphur   fertilizers, paints, detergents, explosives, matches

Talc   powder, paint, rubber, paper

Titanium   metal products, whitener in paints, toothpaste

Tungsten   metal products, lightbulb filaments, dyes

Zinc   rust inhibitor for steel used in cars, buildings, bridges

We give the rocks and minerals that we wear unique names. Some gemstones you can wear are dust pearls, flash opals, green starstones, Montana jets, pigeon blood agates, volcanic glass, and zebra stones.

Talking Temperatures

How hot is it outside? How cold is the water in the pool? The answer might depend on where you live. In Canada, Europe, Asia, and most of the rest of the world, people use the Celsius (or centigrade) scale. In the U.S., most people use the Fahrenheit scale to measure temperature. In the World and Weather section of this book, we gave temperature readings in both scales. Here's the scoop on these two important ways for your mom to find out just how much to insist on your wearing a sweater to school.

CELSIUS

Invented by: Anders Celsius of Sweden in the 1740s

Freezing: $0°$

Body temperature: $37°$

Water boils: $100°$

FAHRENHEIT

Invented by: Gabriel Daniel Fahrenheit of Germany in 1720

Freezing: $32°$

Body temperature: $98.6°$

Water boils: $212°$

TEMPERATURE CONVERSIONS

To convert $X°$ Celsius to the Fahrenheit scale:
Multiply X by 9; divide by 5; then add 32.

To convert $X°$ Fahrenheit to the Celsius scale:
Subtract 32 from X; multiply by 5; then divide by 9.

Celsius was actually an astronomer, not a chemist or physicist. He gained great fame in his day for his many observations about the world and the heavens. He was involved with determining the real shape of Earth and with discovering the magnetic causes of the aurora borealis, the famous "northern lights."

How Loud Is Loud?

Turn down the music, do you want to go deaf? How many times have you heard (or should we say, not heard) that demand? Now you have some research to back you up when you crank the tunes. Sounds are measured using decibels, or "db" for short. Hearing noise of 100 dbs or more over several hours can hurt your ears, so wear ear protection in those cases.

Barely Audible
Breathing	10
Rustling leaves	20
Whispering	20

Very Quiet
Quiet conversation	30
Phone conversation	50

Quiet
Restaurant conversation	60

Loud
Noisy classroom	70
Vacuum cleaner	70

Possible Hearing Damage
Garbage disposal	80

Hearing Damage After Eight Hours
Busy urban street	90
Food blender	90

Extremely Loud
Jackhammer	100
Power lawn mower	100
Motorcycle	100
Car horn	110
Live rock music	120

Threshold of Pain
Jet takeoff *	130
Aircraft carrier deck	140

Physical Pain
Jet takeoff **	150
Rocket engine	180

* from 100 m (110 yards)   ** from 25 m (27.5 yards)

Though it's not spelled the same way, the term *decibel* is actually named after Alexander Graham Bell, the inventor of the telephone. The term means one-tenth ("deci") of one bel, a measurement of sound intensity.

Women in Science

For centuries women were not encouraged or allowed to take part in the study of science. Hypatia and St. Hildegard, below, are two early exceptions. This list features women who made key contributions to science. Imagine what we might have learned if women had been in the labs sooner!

SCIENTIST/LIFE SPAN	WORK
Maude Abbott/1869-1940	One of first female doctors in Canada; expert in heart disease
Elizabeth Blackwell/1821–1910	First female medical doctor in the United States
Rachel Carson/1907–1964	Leader in public awareness of environmental issues
Marie Curie/1867–1934	Researched radioactive elements and compounds
Carrie Derick/1862-1941	Canada's first female university professor
Isobel Dunbar/1918-1999	Expert on Arctic sea ice; first woman on Canadian icebreakers
Jane Goodall/1934–	Studies chimpanzee behavior
Caroline Herschel/1750–1848	Astronomer and first woman to discover a comet
St. Hildegard of Bingen/1098–1179	Wrote about using plants and animals in medicine
Dorothy Crowfoot Hodgkin/1910–1994	Biochemist who worked with penicillin and insulin
Grace Hopper/1906–1992	Invented the computer language COBOL
Hypatia/370–415	Egyptian who was first female mathematician
Elizabeth MacGill/1905–1980	Pioneering Canadian aeronautical engineer
Ruth Ella Moore/1903–1994	Biochemist, did research in blood grouping
Agnes Fay Morgan/1884–1968	Researched vitamins and nutrition
Ann Haven Morgan/1928–	Zoologist who researches human and animal behaviour
Florence Nightingale/1820–1910	Nurse and founder of modern nursing
Edith Hinckley Quimby/1891–1982	Discovered how to use radiation for cancer treatments
Florence Rena Sabin/1871–1953	Worked to cure tuberculosis and to improve sanitation
Roger Arliner Young/1889–1964	A biologist, first black female scientist to publish research

Marie Curie is one of the few people — and the only woman — to win two Nobel Prizes. She won in 1903 for physics and in 1911 for chemistry. She discovered the radioactive element radium in 1898.

Famous Hoaxes

A hoax is something created to fool people. Over the years, many people have "discovered" things that thrilled and excited the scientific community — until those things were proven to be hoaxes. Here are some of the most well-known hoaxes in science history.

The Feejee Mermaid, 1842
Fake: A man showed up in New York with a creature he called a mermaid. Famous showman P. T. Barnum put the mermaid on display and attracted thousands of visitors.
Fact: Barnum had hired the man to create the mermaid, which appeared to be the dead body of a monkey attached to the tail of a fish.

The Cardiff Giant, 1869
Fake: The fossilized body of an ancient man more than 3 m (10 feet) tall was found on a farm in Wales, in Great Britain.
Fact: The "man" was really a stone statue buried by pranksters.

The Piltdown Man, 1911
Fake: A half-million-year-old skull was found in Piltdown, England.
Fact: The skull was 50,000 years old, but the jawbone was only about a decade old. Forgers had built the "prehistoric" skull to fool the public.

The Human Clone, 1978
Fake: A well-known science writer's book revealed that a millionaire had successfully had himself cloned.
Fact: No such cloning took place; in fact, no human has ever been cloned.

The Stone Age Tasadays, 1978
Fake: A Philippine scientist revealed to the world a tribe of people, the Tasadays, who still lived a Stone Age existence.
Fact: The scientist had paid several local tribes, who lived in huts, farmed, and were fairly modern, to pose as the "lost" tribe.

Shinichi Fujimara's Rocks, 2000
Fake: The famous archaeologist "discovered" stone tools he said were more than 600,000 years old.
Fact: Fujimara later admitted burying the tools himself.

People often want to believe amazing stories. When Barnum could not buy the Cardiff Giant and put it on display, he built his own. Amazingly, thousands of people came to see this fake version of a fake "man."

Who's on the Net?

The Internet has literally changed the way that billions of people live. Whether that means searching the World Wide Web for information, sending e-mail, or transferring vast sums of money instantly, the Internet is the first communications system to link the whole world tightly together. Not surprisingly, among the countries that use the Internet (and pretty much all of them do in some way), Canada ranks high on the list of total users, as well as having one of the highest percentages of people on the Internet (see page 221).

COUNTRY	RANK	COUNTRY	RANK
United States	1	France	9
China	2	Russia	10
Japan	3	Canada	11
Germany	4	Brazil	12
India	5	Indonesia	13
United Kingdom	6	Spain	14
South Korea	7	Australia	15
Italy	8	Mexico	16

The percentage of people in Canada with access to the Internet has skyrocketed. In 1998, 36 percent of Canadians were online. By 2003, that number was 64 percent!

The Science of Me

Your body is a walking science lab. You're using dozens of chemicals, many muscles, and important physical forces just to read this sentence. This page is a quick way to keep track of some of your vital statistics, as the doctors call them. You might need a tape measure and a scale for some of them.

My birthday _____

My age in years _____

My age in months _____

My hair colour _____

My eye colour _____

My height in metres, centimetres _____

My weight in kilograms _____

My shoe size _____

My head size _____

My doctor's name _____

My dentist's name _____

If I could be a scientist, I'd be a _____
(see page 126 for ideas)

How many people do you have to have in one room for there to be a 50-50 chance that at least two people will have the same birthday? Answer: Surprise — it's only 30. Try it with a group of your friends or your classmates.

CHAPTER SIX

Words

Without words, this would be nothing but a book of pictures. Of course, that might not be a bad thing, but it would make the lists harder to figure out. This chapter is all about the words we use to communicate.

World Languages

Language is what we use to communicate. It allows people to talk to one another and share thoughts and ideas. A common language allows human beings to work together. It also made civilization possible. Without language for communication, this sentence might read like this: "   ."

LANGUAGE	PRIMARY COUNTRIES	SPEAKERS (IN MILLIONS)
Mandarin Chinese	China	885
Spanish	Spain, Mexico	332
English	Canada, U.S., U.K.*	322
Bengali	Bangladesh	189
Hindi	India	182
Portuguese	Portugal, Brazil	170
Russian	Russia	170
Japanese	Japan	125
German	Germany	98
Wu Chinese	China	77
Javanese	Indonesia	75
Korean	North and South Korea	75
French	France, Canada	72
Vietnamese	Vietnam	67
Telugu	India	66
Cantonese Chinese	China	66

* United Kingdom (Great Britain)

Canada has two official languages: English and French. While the majority of Canadians speak English, more than 6 million speak French. Most French speakers live in Quebec.

Extinct Languages

Some languages, like some animals, have disappeared over the centuries. These extinct languages (and there are hundreds more) might have been swallowed up by a language spoken by a much larger population, or perhaps the people who spoke these languages died out — or in some cases were killed off. In many countries, programs exist to try to make sure that today's languages don't disappear like these have.

LANGUAGE	COUNTRY, LAST YEARS SPOKEN
Gureng Gureng	Australia, unknown*
Wuliwuli	Australia, unknown*
Itene	Bolivia, 1970
Guana	Brazil, unknown*
Dalmatian	Croatia, late 1800s
Coptic	Egypt, 1500s
Geez	Ethiopia, unknown*
Shuadit	France, 1977
Ancient Greek	Greece, unknown*
Skepi Creole Dutch	Guyana, 1998
Ancient Hebrew	Israel, unknown*
Omurano	Peru, 1958
Prussian	Poland, early 1700s
Guanche	Spain, 1500s
Gothic	Ukraine, 1700s
Manx	Isle of Man, 20th century
Powhatan	United States, 1977
Natchez	United States, unknown*

* These languages are ancient, and it is not recorded exactly when the last speakers died.

There are more than 6,800 languages spoken in the world today, and 417 of them are classified as nearly extinct. They are called that when only a few speakers, mostly elderly people, are still living.

How to Count in Other Languages
Uno to Shi

Here's a handy chart for the numbers 1 to 10 in six major languages. Check out how similar the sounds are for some numbers (7, for instance) even though the languages are very different and come from all over the world.

NO.	SPANISH	FRENCH	GERMAN	ARABIC#	SWAHILI	CHINESE**
1	uno	un	eins	wahid	moia	yi
2	dos	deux	zwei	ithnin	mbili	er
3	tres	trois	drei	thalatha	tatu	san
4	quatro	quatre	vier	arba	nne	si
5	cinco	cinq	fünf	khamsa	tano	wu
6	seis	six	sechs	sitta	sita	liu
7	siete	sept	sieben	saba	saba	qi
8	ocho	huit	acht	thamania	nane	ba
9	nueve	neuf	neun	tisa	tisa	jiu
10	diez	dix	zehn	ashra	kumi	shi

These languages use non-Western characters that are pronounced with these sounds.
* Mandarin Chinese

French and Spanish are part of the "Romance" language family, meaning they came from Latin, the language of ancient Rome. Latin also gave us the names of some months of the year, based on how the Romans counted months. In the Roman calendar, September, October, November, and December were months 7 through 10. Take off the "ber" and you've got the Latin numbers for 7 through 10.

Thanks, World

It is one of the most polite things you can say. Your parent or teacher probably reminds you to say it 20 times a day. You can use it in almost any situation. Next time you have to say thank you, try one of these on for size.

PHRASE	LANGUAGE	HOW TO SAY IT
Asante	Swahili	ah-SANT-ay
Danke	German	DAHNK-uh
Domo arigato	Japanese	DOH-moh ar-ee-GAHT-oh
Dziekuje	Polish	zeh-KOOJ-uh
Efcharisto	Greek	ef-har-EES-toh
Gracias	Spanish	GRA-see-ahs
Grazie	Italian	GRA-tzee
Kiitos	Finnish	KIH-tos
Köszönöm	Hungarian	KEHS-seh-nem
Mahalo	Hawaiian	mah-HAH-low
Merci	French	mare-SEE
Obrigado	Portuguese	oh-bree-GAH-doh
Salamat	Tagalog	sah-LAH-maht
Shoukran	Arabic	show-KROHN
Spasibo	Russian	spahs-EE-boh
Tack	Swedish	TOK
Tesekkur	Turkish	tehs-eh-KUR
Todah	Hebrew	TOE-dah

On the **TV** show and in the movie series *Star Trek*, how do the characters from the planet Vulcan and Klingon say thank you? (The show's producers created vocabularies for these imaginary planets, and many fans learned to speak the "languages.")

Answer: Vulcan: Neimaayo; Klingon: Tlho'.

Dots and Hands

Letters, words, and speech are just a few of the many ways we communicate with other people. Here are two systems of communication that you can use. On this page is Morse code, invented by Samuel Morse in 1840 when he perfected the telegraph. This system transmitted electronic sounds — called dots and dashes, that is, a short click for a dot and a longer click for dash — over long distances across wires. American Sign Language (ASL) is used by deaf people in the U.S. and English Canada. French Canadians speak *Le langage des signes québécois*. Both of these languages use the manual alphabet on the opposite page to spell out individual words and names, in addition to the signs and gestures that make up their language.

LETTER	MORSE CODE	LETTER	MORSE CODE
A	· –	O	– – –
B	– · · ·	P	· – – ·
C	– · – ·	Q	– – · –
D	– · ·	R	· – ·
E	·	S	· · ·
F	· · – ·	T	–
G	– – ·	U	· · –
H	· · · ·	V	· · · –
I	· ·	W	· – –
J	· – – –	X	– · · –
K	– · –	Y	– · – –
L	· – · ·	Z	– – · ·
M	– –	Period	· – · – · –
N	– ·	Comma	– – · · – –

THE MANUAL ALPHABET

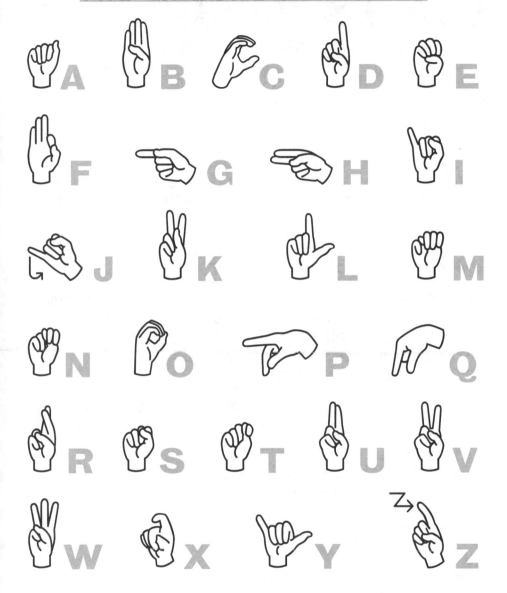

American Sign Language is not an adaptation of spoken or written English — the grammar is not at all similar. And ASL is completely different from British Sign Language.

Parts of Speech

The parts of speech are the classification of words according to how they are used in a sentence. In English, there are eight parts of speech. But, of course, you know that already since you've paid so much attention in English class, right?

Adjectives descriptive words; usually modify nouns.
EXAMPLES: big, sweet, beautiful

Adverbs words that modify verbs or adjectives, often end in "ly". EXAMPLES: wildly, brightly, beautifully

Conjunctions connecting words that link sentences and phrases. EXAMPLES: and, but, because, as

Interjections either stand-alone words or words that are thrown into a sentence without becoming a part of the structure of the sentence. They express surprise, excitement, or some other strong emotion or feeling.
EXAMPLES: hello! yikes! ouch! oh, my!

Nouns word used to name a person, place, thing, idea, or action. EXAMPLES: book, rocket, science, call (as in "make a call")

Prepositions connecting words that show the relationship or position of one word or thing to another.
EXAMPLES: of, over, under, beside, for

Pronouns words that take the place of nouns.
EXAMPLES: he, she, it, they, himself

Verbs words that express action.
EXAMPLES: run, eat, poke, spit, scream

Can you think of some sentences that have only one word in them? Here's a hint: You always need a verb to make a sentence . . . but you don't need a noun or pronoun.

Answers: Some choices are "Go," "Eat," "Wait," and "Run!" You probably thought of others, too.

Punctuation Marks

Just as traffic signs govern the rules of the road, punctuation marks help you follow the rules of writing. For example, all drivers stop at a red light, and all readers stop at a period. Look, here comes one now. A yellow blinking light means slow down, much like a comma, like that one or this one, which serves as a breather for the reader.

' **Apostrophe** shows possession (or missing letters)

[ ] **Brackets** enclose a category or group of thoughts

: **Colon** used to introduce an example, explanation, or series

, **Comma** marks separation within the sentence

— **Dash** indicates a break in thought

... **Ellipsis** shows a thought continues or words are missing

! **Exclamation point** shows emphasis and strong feeling

- **Hyphen** joins words

( ) **Parentheses** provide added information or an aside

. **Period** ends a sentence

? **Question mark** asks a direct question

" " **Quotation marks** identify speech or special words

; **Semicolon** links major elements of a sentence

PSSST You can also use punctuation to create little sideways "faces" on your computer. They're called emoticons. Some examples: :-) [happy] and :-([sad] and ;-) [winking face] and :-o [surprised]. What others can you create?

Forms of Poetry

Usually, poetry is thought of as a written art, but poetry began before writing, in prehistoric times. People used a kind of poetic language in songs, prayers, and magic spells. The rhyming patterns helped storytellers and others to remember the words. Lyric poetry usually deals with feelings, emotions, and the senses. Narrative poems are more focused on telling stories.

LYRIC POETRY

Haiku a Japanese form with 17 syllables — five syllables in the first line, seven in the second, and five in the third

Ode a form that marks a serious event, gives high praise, or is about noble feelings

Elegy a meditation on life and death

Sonnet a 14-line love poem

Limerick a five-line form of humorous verse (see below)

NARRATIVE POETRY

Epic a lengthy poem that describes an historic and/or heroic event

Ballad a shorter story about a particular person

DRAMATIC POETRY

Dramatic poets tell stories through many characters, much like a playwright. If a play's dialogue has many rhymes, the play is considered to be dramatic poetry. English playwright William Shakespeare is the most famous dramatic poet.

PsSST

There once was a book made of lists.
'Twas so heavy I 'bout broke my wrists.
But I read it all through
Till I knew what to do,
And I had more good grades in my fists.

Forms of Prose

Prose (rhymes with *nose*) is any writing that is not poetry. Newspapers are prose. This book is filled with prose. Most of the books you read are in some form of prose. There are many types of prose, however, and here are some of the ones you might run into.

FICTION

Fable uses characters to convey a simple message
Fairy tale adventure in which heroes win over evil
Fantasy set in an imaginary world with imaginary characters
Historical fiction story based on history, with fictional main characters
Horror stories about scary things
Mystery stories, often involving crime, in which the characters search for something
Myth a story made up to explain real events or about gods and godesses of ancient cultures
Romance stories in which the characters look for love
Science fiction futuristic stories that use elements of modern science
Tall tales humorous stories that are full of exaggeration

NONFICTION

Autobiography a story of the author's life
Biography a story of a person's life written by someone else
Essay nonfiction story that discusses one topic
History an account of a past event or era
Journal a diary or record of day-to-day events
News stories reports about events of the recent past
Reference a collection of useful facts and information

This is an easy one. What form of prose is the *Scholastic Canada Book of Lists*?

Answer: Fantasy! No, just kidding. It's reference.

A Writer's Toolbox

Writers have many ways to express their thoughts. Without knowing it, you probably use some of these popular tools in your own writing. Work with your teacher to try out one or two of these that you haven't used before.

Alliteration   repetition of the same sound at the beginning of two or more words

Allusion   something talked about through hints

Assonance   words that have the same vowel sound

Characters   the people or creatures in a story

Climax   the high point of a story, usually just before the ending

Dialogue   conversation between two or more characters

Hyperbole   extreme exaggeration used to express an idea or opinion

Imagery   words that help form pictures in readers' minds

Irony   says one thing but has a second, usually opposite, meaning

Metaphor   comparison of different things to show likeness

Mood   the feeling of a story; can be sad, happy, gloomy, scary, etc.

Onomatopoeia   invented words that imitate real sounds

Plot   the actions or events that drive a story forward

Setting   the time and location in which the story takes place

Simile   a figure of speech that compares two different things

 Without onomatopoeia (on-ah-maht-ah-PEA-ah), comic-book characters could not go "POW!" "ZAP!" "WHAM!" or "ZING!" See if you can make up a word to describe a real sound.

Biggest Newspapers

While TV and the Internet provide a great deal of world news, newspapers remain among the most important and respected sources of information. Here is a list of the top newspapers in Canada, ranked by circulation (how many copies are sold every day), as well as a list of top international newspapers.

CANADA

NEWSPAPER	CITY	CIRCULATION
Toronto Star	Toronto	440,654
The Globe and Mail	National	314,178
Le Journal de Montreal	Montreal	267,194
National Post	National	246,504
Toronto Sun	Toronto	208,429
La Presse	Montreal	188,693

WORLD

NEWSPAPER	COUNTRY	CIRCULATION
Yomiuri Shimbun	Japan	14,407,000
Asahi Shimbun	Japan	12,393,000
Mainichi Shimbun	Japan	5,685,000
Nihon Keizai Shimbun	Japan	4,703,000
Chunichi Shimbun	Japan	4,635,000
Bild	Germany	4,390,000

The first newspaper published on a regular basis in Canada was the *Halifax Gazette,* which started publication on March 23, 1752.

Homonyms

English can be a puzzling language. It's filled with many confusing words, such as homonyms. These are words that sound the same but have different meanings. A dictionary can help you sort out the meanings of each of these word pairs. Here are some homonyms that you might trip over.

allowed	aloud	meat	meet
bare	bear	pair	pear
blew	blue	peace	piece
brake	break	plain	plane
colonel	kernel	pray	prey
dear	deer	right	write
fair	fare	role	roll
feat	feet	sail	sale
flour	flower	soar	sore
hear	here	son	sun
heard	herd	stair	stare
hole	whole	tail	tale
hour	our	threw	through
know	no	waist	waste
loan	lone	wait	weight
mail	male	way	weigh
main	mane	weak	week

There are even some "triple" homonyms. Some examples of these are to, too, two; their, there, they're; rain, rein, reign; cent, sent, scent.

Contractions

A contraction is a word made up of two words combined into one by leaving out one or more letters. An apostrophe appears in place of the missing letters. Here is a list of common contractions and their meanings.

CONTRACTION	MEANING	CONTRACTION	MEANING
aren't	are not	she'll	she will
can't	cannot	she's	she is, she has
couldn't	could not	shouldn't	should not
could've	could have	should've	should have
didn't	did not	there'll	there will
doesn't	does not	there's	there is
don't	do not	they'll	they will
hadn't	had not	they're	they are
hasn't	has not	they've	they have
haven't	have not	'tis	it is
he'd	he would	'twas	it was
he'll	he will	wasn't	was not
he's	he is, he has	we'd	we would
I'd	I would	we'll	we will
I'll	I will	we're	we are
I'm	I am	weren't	were not
isn't	is not	we've	we have
it'll	it will	what's	what is
it's	it is	won't	will not
I've	I have	wouldn't	would not
let's	let us	would've	would have
mightn't	might not	you'll	you will
might've	might have	you're	you are
mustn't	must not	you've	you have

One set of words often trips up writers: the difference between "it's" and "its." The first is indeed a contraction, short for "it is." The second is a possessive pronoun.

Abbreviations

Abbreviations make words shorter by leaving out letters. The letters that are left mean the same thing that the longer original word did. Periods are sometimes used to show an abbreviation.

A.I.	artificial intelligence		**FYI**	for your information
a.k.a	also known as		**i.e.**	that is (Latin: *id est*)
A.M.	morning (Latin: *ante meridien*)		**IQ**	Intelligence Quotient
			Jr.	Junior
ASAP	as soon as possible		**k.p.h.**	kilometres per hour
asst.	assistant		**lb.**	pound (from the Latin *libra*, for scale)
ave.	avenue			
blvd.	boulevard		**M.D.**	medical doctor
co.	company		**Messrs.**	plural of Mr.
CPR	cardiopulmonary resuscitation		**oz.**	ounce (from the Italian word *onza*)
dept.	department		**PC**	politically correct
Dr.	doctor		**P.M.**	afternoon (Latin: *post meridien*)
DVD	digital video disc			
e.g.	for example (Latin: *exempli gratia*)		**PS**	postscript, at end of a letter
ESP	extrasensory perception		**Sr.**	Senior
			TBA	to be announced
ETA	estimated time of arrival		**TBD**	to be determined
			TLC	tender loving care
et al.	and others (Latin: *et alia*)		**UFO**	unidentified flying object
etc.	and so forth (Latin: *et cetera*)		**VCR**	video cassette recorder

RSVP is an abbreviation you've probably seen. It stands for the French phrase "répondez s'il-vous-plaît," which means "please reply" in English.

Palindromes—semordnilaP

A palindrome is a word or phrase that reads the same forward and backward. The result is often kind of funny. See if you can make up palindromes of your own.

WORDS

mom

dad

noon

tot

bob

pop

race car

toot

sees

level

radar

PHRASES

Madam, I'm Adam.

Step on no pets.

Bald elf fled lab.

No panic, I nap on!

Ed is loopy poolside.

Ma's story rots, Sam.

No lemons, no melon.

Rats live on no evil star.

No way a papaya won!

Elk rap song? No sparkle.

Lee has a race car as a heel.

Some men interpret nine memos.

Go hang a salami, I'm a lasagna hog.

A man, a plan, a cat, a bar, a cap, a mall, a ball, a map, a car, a bat, a canal: Panama.

If you love palindromes (or if your name is Otto or Eve), check out *Too Hot to Hoot: Funny Palindrome Riddles* by Marvin Terban. It's all about these fun words and phrases.

Misspeled Wurds

Or should we say "Misspelled Words"? Spelling, no matter what anyone tells you, is important. If you don't spell words correctly, you risk having people misunderstand what you're writing. Spelling in English often can be done by sounding out words. However, here are just a few of the words that aren't spelled the way they sound and often trip up even good spellers.

answer
broccoli
business
chief
committee
cough
debt
desperate
disappear
doctor
dumb
eighth
enough
exaggerate
exercise
February
gauge
guess

half
league
licence
minute
misspell
necessary
neighbour
often
once
scissors
separate
their
through
truly
vacuum
Wednesday
where
whole

PsSST

In 2005, Finola Hackett of Edmonton won the first CanWest CanSpell Cup, a spelling bee, by correctly spelling the word otiosity—which means laziness!

Tongue Twisters

A tongue twister is a phrase that is difficult to pronounce. The words are difficult to speak rapidly because of a succession of similar sounds (which is actually sort of a tongue twister itself). See how fast you can say these. For extra credit, say them fast over and over.

Sam shaved seven shy sheep.

Nat's knapsack strap snapped.

A proper copper coffeepot.

Fred's friend Fran flips fine flapjacks fast.

She sells seashells by the seashore.

**If Peter Piper picked a peck of
    pickled peppers,
How many pickled peppers would
    Peter Piper pick?**

**A skunk sat on a stump.
The stump thunk the skunk stunk.
The skunk thunk the stump stunk.**

**A tutor who tooted a flute
Tried to tutor two tooters to toot.
Said the two to their tutor,
"Is it harder to toot or
To tutor two tooters to toot?"**

**Actors sometimes use tongue twisters to
loosen up their mouths and vocal cords
before a performance. One of their exercises
is to say "toy boat" several times very
quickly. See how many times you can say it.**

Worn-out Words

Words that are superpopular today might seem like another language to kids 100 years from now (heck, they might be gone next summer). Words go out of fashion, they stop being used, or they're replaced by other words. Here are some words and phrases that your parents or grandparents probably thought would be around forever. They were wrong!

WORD	MEANING
bloomers	ladies' underwear
the bee's knees	phrase for "cool"
countenance	face
dapper	describes a fancy dresser
forbearance	patience
gentleman caller	a boyfriend
knickers	kids' short pants
rantipole	wild or unruly
settee	small sofa
shan't	"shall not" (will not)
spectacles	eyeglasses
steamer	cruise ship
thither	over there
thole	suffer or bear
thou	you
ye	the
Zounds!	expression of surprise

So now you know what this means:
"Thou will need forbeareance to thole ye gentleman caller, even if he is the bee's knees."

Prefixes and Suffixes

A prefix is a letter or group of letters at the beginning of a word that contributes to the word's meaning. Suffixes come at the end of words and affect the meaning of the whole word by combining with the "root" word.

PREFIX	MEANING	SUFFIX	MEANING
anti-	against	**-able, -ible**	capable of
astro-	star	**-ant, -ent**	like, similar
atmo-	vapour, gas	**-ation**	action, state, result
bi-	two	**-dom**	condition of
co-, com-, con-	with, together with	**-en**	made of, like
		-ess	feminine
contra-	contrary to	**-ful**	full of
de-	down, away from	**-fuge**	away from
dis-	not, off, away	**-gamy**	marriage
ex-	out, from, former	**-gon**	angle
extra-	outside	**-hood**	state of
for-	away, off, from	**-ish**	like, pertaining to
fore-	before, previous	**-ism**	practice of
non-	not	**-less**	without
omni-	all	**-ly**	in the nature of
ped-	foot	**-ment**	act of
pedi-	child	**-meter**	instrument
post-	after	**-ness**	state of
pre-	before	**-ory, -ary**	relating
sub-	under, beneath	**-ous, -ose**	full of
un-	not	**-ward**	in the direction of

Latin is the source of many of the dozens of prefixes and suffixes in English. Words from that language can be called called "Latinate," which has a suffix itself — "-ate," which means having or showing.

My Words

This chapter was about words and letters and languages. Here's a place for you to make lists of words that are important to you. For "what my last name means," you can ask your parents or do some research. Names can tell a lot about a family's history. Some are based on your ancestor's profession, or on where they lived, or on what clan or family they came from. Your first name might have a meaning in another language, too.

My full name _____

My nickname _____

What I wish my
nickname was _____

A cute name my
family calls me _____

What my friends
call me _____

What my last name
means _____

Three words that
describe me _____

_____

_____

Languages that I speak _____

Languages that I'd like
to learn _____

Three words that you
can make up using the
letters in my name _____

_____

_____

CHAPTER SEVEN

The Arts

There is more to "art" than just drawing on your walls and making papier-mâché statues. Painting, sculpture, music, dance, and even architecture are all part of "the arts."

Art Periods

Like any work of art, the history of art itself is subject to people's opinions. Dating exactly when periods ended or began is open to debate. But here's a rough time line showing the different periods of art history from the prehistoric to the present.

Prehistoric
from dramatic cave art 25,000 to 35,000 years ago to the days around 2000 B.C.

Ancient
including Egyptian, Greek, and Roman art dating to a few hundred years A.D.

Medieval
early Christian, Roman, Gothic, and Byzantine art to the mid-15th century

Renaissance
the cultural revolution in Italy from 1480 to 1527

Northern Renaissance
in European countries north of Italy in the late 15th and 16th centuries

Mannerism
in post-Renaissance Italy in the 16th century

Baroque
the late 16th and 17th centuries in Europe

Rococo
the dominant style of the 18th century in Europe

Neoclassicism and Romanticism
these styles flourished in the late 18th and early 19th centuries in Europe

Impressionism
early to late 19th century; started in Europe

Postimpressionism
late 19th century to the early 20th century; started in Europe

Modern Art
since the early 20th century worldwide

For more information on some of these styles, please see page 184.

The Italian Renaissance spawned much of the classic art — such as works by Leonardo da Vinci, Raphael, and Michelangelo — that is familiar even to people who know little about the rest of the art world.

Famous Too Late

Many great artists do not become famous during their lifetimes. Sometimes it can be many decades or even centuries before their genius is recognized. While they don't get to enjoy all the fame and money their art eventually earns, at least they can "know" that millions of people are able to enjoy the works of art they created. Here are a trio of artists whose fame skyrocketed only after their deaths.

Vincent van Gogh

Around the turn of the 20th century, you could buy an original painting by Vincent van Gogh for as little as five cents in a marketplace in the Netherlands. Van Gogh was all but ignored in his field during his lifetime; it wasn't until long after his death, at age 37, in 1890 that his paintings received praise and became very valuable.

Paul Gauguin

Gauguin was so hurt by the criticism his work received in Europe in the late 1800s that he sailed to Tahiti, where he produced some of his finest paintings. But in 1903, he died — alone and penniless — in the Marquesas Islands.

Henri Rousseau

Rousseau made a living at various jobs, including as a toll collector for the city of Paris, earning him the nickname, "The Customs Official." As an artist, he was self-taught, and his work was dismissed by much of the art community. He was buried in a pauper's grave after his death in 1910.

One hundred years after Vincent Van Gogh's death, his *Portrait of Dr. Gachet* was auctioned for a record $99 million.

Name That Art!

What kinds of art are there? You've got sculpture, painting, drawing, and more. Art experts, however, use many other terms to describe types of art. These terms are used when talking about styles and movements of art from the past two millennia.

Abstract
little or no reference to realistic appearance or natural objects

Baroque
ornate and elaborate art of the late 16th century and all of the 17th century

Byzantine
religious art that emerged from the early Christian world

Cubism
rearranges natural forms through different shapes and colours

Dadaism
unconventional art movement that avoided traditional art forms

Fauvism
conflicting and intense colours and images

Impressionism
captures the impression of a subject and shows how it is affected by sunlight

Neoclassicism
modelled on traditional Greek and Roman art

Pop
utilizes images from popular culture

Postimpressionism
an extension of Impressionism that bridged the gap to modern art

Realism
portrays ordinary people in everyday situations

Romanticism
emotional and graphic art created to be the opposite of Neoclassicism

Surrealism
portrays alternate realities, including dreams and fantasy

Dadaism comes from the French word "dada," which means hobbyhorse. It was chosen randomly out of a dictionary in 1916 at a meeting of artists in Switzerland.

Most Expensive Art

Going once . . . going twice . . . sold! Paintings are some of the most valuable pieces of art in the world. Collectors and museums pay big bucks for the right to own these paintings and hang them in their homes or galleries. These paintings are the most expensive works of art ever sold on the auction block.

PAINTING (ARTIST, YEAR SOLD)	PRICE (CAN$)
Portrait of Dr. Gachet **Vincent van Gogh, 1990**	**$99,600,000**
Au Moulin de la Galette **Pierre-Auguste Renoir, 1990**	**$94,200,000**
Portrait de l'artiste sans barbe **Vincent van Gogh, 1998**	**$86,300,000**
Still Life with Curtain **Paul Cézanne, 1999**	**$73,000,000**
Les Noces de Pierrette **Pablo Picasso, 1989**	**$62,400,000**
Irises **Vincent van Gogh, 1987**	**$59,200,000**
Le Rêve **Pablo Picasso, 1997**	**$53,100,000**
Self-portrait: Yo Picasso **Pablo Picasso, 1989**	**$52,500,000**
Au Lapin Agile **Pablo Picasso, 1989**	**$44,600,000**
Sunflowers **Vincent van Gogh, 1987**	**$43,700,000**

More than 200 of legendary Spanish artist Pablo Picasso's paintings have sold for $1 million or more.

Odd Art

In art, beauty is in the eye of the beholder. After all, where else is one man's shovel another man's work of art? Here are several well-known works of art that can be described as "off the wall."

Campbell's Soup I (Tomato)
By Andy Warhol

Warhol became famous in the 1960s for his paintings of products such as Coca-Cola bottles and Brillo pads, and of celebrities such as Marilyn Monroe and Jackie Onassis. Perhaps his most recognizable work is this painting of a solitary can of Campbell's tomato soup.

In Advance of the Broken Arm
By Marcel Duchamp

Duchamp's works are some of the best examples of Dadaism (see page 184). This piece was simply a snow shovel presented as art. Critics coined it "ready-made" art.

Surrounded Islands
By Christo and Jeanne-Claude

Christo and Jeanne-Claude wrapped 11 islands in Biscayne Bay, Florida, with bright pink fabric. The couple's outdoor sculptures often included surrounding or wrapping huge objects in canvas or other types of sheeting. Among their other works: wrapping the German Reichstag (government building) and the Pont Neuf (a bridge) in Paris.

Whaam!
By Roy Lichtenstein

Like Andy Warhol, Lichtenstein was a leader in the pop-art movement of the 1960s. His paintings drew heavily from commercial products and advertising. He is best known for paintings, such as *Whaam!*, that were done in comic-book style.

Marcel Duchamp earned additional notoriety in 1920 with *La Joconde aux Mustaches* — a reproduction of the *Mona Lisa* with a beard and mustache painted on her face!

Colour Your World

Colour is one of the artist's main tools for creating different looks or effects. The possibilities multiply as the artist mixes primary colours, then secondary and tertiary colours.

Primary colours are the basic colours and can't be made by mixing any other colours.
- Blue • Red • Yellow

Secondary colours are made by mixing primary colours.
- Green (mix blue/yellow)
- Orange (mix red/yellow)
- Violet (mix blue/red)

Tertiary colours, also known as intermediate colours, are made by mixing a primary colour with a secondary colour.
- Blue-green • Blue-violet
- Yellow-green • Yellow-orange
- Red-orange • Red-violet

Colours of the rainbow
- Red • Orange • Yellow
- Green • Blue • Indigo • Violet

PsSST To remember a rainbow's colours in order, think of the name Roy G. Biv. Those letters match up with the first letters of the colours.

Musical Terms

Like painting, archaeology, and teenagers, music has a language all its own. Specialized terms are used to describe different parts of how music sounds, how music is made (or "composed"), or how people sound when they're singing. Many of these terms come from Latin or Italian. If you don't know an alto from a soprano or a baritone from a tenor, here's your chance to learn a few basic musical terms.

A cappella music performed without instrumental accompaniment

Alto low, female singing voice

Aria solo song accompanied by an orchestra, as in an opera

Baritone male singing voice higher than a bass but lower than a tenor

Bass low, male singing voice

Beat basic unit of time in music

Bridge the musical transition between two parts of a composition

Chord three or more notes sounded simultaneously

Crescendo music that gradually grows louder and/or more intense

Encore an additional performance requested by extended applause from the audience

Falsetto high male singing voice, produced above the normal range

Harmony the simultaneous combination of notes in a chord

Libretto the text of an opera

Measure rhythm grouping that contains a fixed number of beats

Melody closely related sequence of single tones that are heard as a unit

Mere organization of music into measures or bars

Overture introductory music for an opera or other long musical work

Refrain verse that is repeated throughout a song

Rhythm the regulated movement of music in time

Scale an ascending or descending series of tones

Soprano the highest natural human singing voice, usually found in women or young boys

Tenor high, male singing voice

Want to hear more music? At the end of a performance, applaud and ask for the encore. Real music fans shout out "Bravo!" to honour the musicians.

Instrumentally Speaking

Instruments can be used to play different styles of music. Violins, for example, are used for classical, country, rock, and jazz. Here are some of the traditional instruments in popular music categories.

COUNTRY
Banjo
Mandolin
Guitar
Fiddle
Organ
Harmonica
Piano

JAZZ
Trumpet
Trombone
Saxophone
Clarinet
Guitar
Bass
Tuba
Drums
Oboe

ROCK 'N' ROLL
Electric guitar
Bass guitar
Drums
Piano or keyboard

Hip-hop and rap musicians depend more on their voices and a turntable than on instruments. What was the first rap/hip-hop song to achieve national hit status?

Answer: *Rapper's Delight*, by the Sugarhill Gang, was released in 1979. Though many people are responsible for creating hip-hop and rap, this was the first hit song.

World Music

In the past few years, music from many parts of the world has become popular in Canada and the United States. There are just about as many types of music as there are countries, but here are the names and home countries of some music you might have heard on the radio or on TV.

MUSIC	HOMELAND	MUSIC	HOMELAND
Bhajan	India	Mariachi	Mexico
Bomba	Puerto Rico	Merengue	Dominican Republic
Cajun	Louisiana, U.S.		
Calypso	Trinidad	Reggae	Jamaica
Celtic	Ireland, Scotland	Rumba	Cuba
		Samba	Brazil
Flamenco	Spain	Slack key guitar	Hawaii
Gamelan	Indonesia	Salsa	New York City*, U.S.
Isicathamiya	S. Africa	Tango	Argentina
Juju	Nigeria	Zouk	Martinique
Kodo	Japan	Zydeco	Louisiana, U.S.

* Developed in the 1950s by people from Puerto Rico who were living in New York.

The Cajun people of Louisiana were originally French Canadians from the region called Acadia. They were kicked out in the 1700s and ended up way down south in "Loos-ee-ana." A mispronunciation of their original home changed Acadia to "Cajun."

Inside the Orchestra

An orchestra is composed of instruments in four families: string, woodwind, brass, and percussion. Here are the members of each family, most of which are found in large orchestras.

STRINGS
Violin
Viola
Cello
Double bass
Harp

WOODWINDS
Flute
Oboe
Clarinet
Bassoon
Piccolo
English horn
E-flat clarinet
Bass clarinet
Contrabassoon

BRASS
French horn
Trumpet
Trombone
Tuba

PERCUSSION
Snare drum
Timpani
Cymbals
Bass drum
Tam-tam
Glockenspiel
Celesta
Maracas
Chimes
Triangle
Castanets
Piano
Xylophone

PsSST Maracas are made from a hollowed gourd, a relative of the squash. The gourd's hard rind is filled with dried seeds or beads that make a rattling sound when the maraca is shaken.

Famous Orchestras

Orchestras are large groups of musicians assembled to play music, usually classical music. For most of the musicians, this a full-time job. Orchestras are led by conductors and music directors; often these people are among the most well-known in the classical music world. Here are a dozen of the world's most famous orchestras.

Academy of St. Martin in the Fields (London, England)
Berlin Philharmonic
Boston Symphony Orchestra
City of Birmingham (England) Symphony Orchestra
London Philharmonic Orchestra
Los Angeles Philharmonic
Moscow Chamber Orchestra
National Symphony Orchestra (Washington, D.C.)
New York Philharmonic
National Arts Centre Orchestra (Ottawa)
Royal Philharmonic Orchestra (London, England)
Vienna Philharmonic

Vienna, Austria, was home to legendary composers **Wolfgang Mozart** and **Ludwig von Beethoven** in the late **1700s** and early **1800s**, but each failed to create a successful orchestra for the city. It wasn't until **1842** — **51** years after the death of Mozart and **15** years after the death of Beethoven — that the Vienna Philharmonic was founded.

Delightful Dancers

Dance is perhaps the most beautiful of the performing arts. Classical ballet and modern dance, which these dance companies specialize in, demand incredible balance, grace, strength, and timing. They can be as athletic as a basketball game, but all set to music. There are thousands of companies dancing on stages and in theatres around the world. Here are some of the most well-known and accomplished.

Alvin Ailey American Dance Theater
American Ballet Theater
Bolshoi Ballet
Joffrey Ballet of Chicago
José Limón Dance Company
Martha Graham Dance Company
Moscow Ballet
National Ballet of Canada
New York City Ballet
Paris Opera Ballet
Royal Ballet (London)

A dancer in the Moscow Ballet goes through about two pairs of shoes per performance. At about 200 performances a year, that adds up to . . . a lot of shoes!

Dance Styles

Gotta dance? Choose your style and hit the floor. Here are some of the most popular and well-known styles of dancing.

African
Asian
Ballet
Ballroom
Belly
Break
Country
Disco
Folk

Hip-hop
Jazz
Latin
Modern
Square
Swing
Tap
Waltz

PsSST

Hip-hop and jazz dancing are obviously very athletic. But ballet can be a real workout, too. A male ballet dancer might have to lift as much as 1,360 kg (1.5 tons) of ballerinas in a single performance (though not all at once, of course).

Famous Broadway Shows

A play or a musical isn't a hit until it's a hit on Broadway. Broadway is the name of the main north–south avenue in New York City. Where it crosses 42nd Street, it forms Times Square. The streets around this intersection are home to dozens of large theatres, all collectively known as Broadway. Here are some of the most popular Broadway shows in history.

42nd Street

A Chorus Line

Annie

Beauty and the Beast

Cabaret

Cats

Chicago

Fiddler on the Roof

Grease

Hair

Hello, Dolly!

Les Misérables

Man of La Mancha

Miss Saigon

My Fair Lady

Oklahoma!

Rent

South Pacific

The Lion King

The Phantom of the Opera

The Producers

When the curtain closed on *Cats* for the final time in September 2000, it ended the show's run of nearly 18 years on Broadway — a record 7,485 performances!

Important Operas

You might not realize it, but opera is one of the world's oldest and most popular forms of theatrical entertainment. The first opera is considered to be *Dafne*, written in 1597. Opera often combines music and emotion like no other art form. Here are some of the most important operas, memorable either for their groundbreaking work or for their popular appeal.

Aida

The Barber of Seville

La Bohème

Boris Godunov

Carmen

Così fan tutte

Dido and Aeneas

Don Giovanni

Fidelio

Madama Butterfly

The Magic Flute

The Marriage of Figaro

Otello

I Pagliacci

Porgy and Bess

Rigoletto

The Ring cycle

La Traviata

Tristan and Isolde

German composer Richard Wagner's Ring cycle is actually a collection of four operas. It took him 27 years to complete the massive work.

Famous Opera Singers

You don't have to be an opera fan (opera fans are called "aficionados") to recognize the names Luciano Pavarotti, Plácido Domingo, and José Carreras — the Three Tenors. Here are some other famous opera singers, past and present.

SINGER	HOME COUNTRY
Cecilia Bartoli	Italy
Maria Callas	Greece
José Carreras	Spain
Enrico Caruso	Italy
Plácido Domingo	Spain
Kirsten Flagstad	Norway
Ben Heppner	Canada
Marilyn Horne	United States
John McCormack	Ireland
Nellie Melba	Australia
Lauritz Melchior	Denmark
Birgit Nilsson	Sweden
Jessye Norman	United States
Luciano Pavarotti	Italy
Leontyne Price	United States
Beverly Sills	United States
Ebe Stignani	Italy
Renata Tebaldi	Italy
Jon Vickers	Canada
Frederica von Stade	United States

PsSST Have you ever eaten melba toast or peach melba? These tasty foods were named for opera singer Dame Nellie Melba, who was very popular in the late 1800s and early 1900s.

Many Voices as One

Some of the most beautiful musical sounds come from choirs or choruses, small or large groups of people singing together as one voice. Here are some of the world's most famous choirs.

CHOIR	HOME CITY
Boys Choir of Harlem	New York City, U.S.
King's College Choir	Cambridge, England
London Chapel Royal Choir	London, England
Mormon Tabernacle Choir	Salt Lake City, U.S.
National Cathedral Choir	Washington, D.C., U.S.
St. Thomas Church Choir	Leipzig, Germany
Sistine Chapel Choir	Vatican City
Vienna Boys Choir	Vienna, Austria

Members of the Vienna Boys Choir wear sailor suits. The tradition started in the 1920s when the choir needed uniforms for singing away from churches. Most boys of the era already owned a sailor suit, which was a popular fashion choice at the time, so that became their standard performance costume, too.

Architectural Styles

Just as music, art, and literature have special words to describe things, architecture also has its own vocabulary. Throughout history, buildings have changed as new materials were created, new ideas were thought up, and new ways of building were invented. Here are just a few of the many architectural styles from which a builder can choose.

Art nouveau	Gothic
Art deco	Greek revival
California ranch	Mission
Cape Cod	Modern
Colonial	Romanesque
Federal	Tudor
Georgian	Victorian

Victorian architecture sometimes involves very elaborate decorations on the outside of houses. The style became popular in England during the reign of Queen Victoria in the 19th century.

Brag About Bricks

The world of architecture is also full of colourful words that describe parts of buildings. For instance, a widow's walk is a rooftop observation deck originally designed to watch for boats returning to port after long voyages. Here are some other terms that you can use to show off your knowledge of the building world.

Baluster
pillar or post that supports a handrail

Campanile
a bell tower often near, but not attached to, a church

Facade
the face of a building

Gable
triangular wall section at the end of a pitched roof

Gargoyle
a rooftop figure carved as a grotesque human or animal

Jamb
vertical posts of a door or window frame

Joist
wall-to-wall beam used to support a floor or ceiling

Lintel
horizontal beam that bridges an opening such as a door frame

Mullion
the vertical post or strip that divides window panes

Niche
recess in a wall, often used for a statue or other ornament

Pergola
trellised walkway in a garden covered by climbing plants

Soffit
the underside of an architectural element

Stanchion
a vertical supporting pole or post

Stud
upright post in a wall for supporting drywall

Transom
a horizontal bar across a window or the top of a door

In Pisa, Italy, there is a building that is perhaps the world's most famous example of a campanile. The building, however, has something odd about it. What is it called?

Answer: The Leaning Tower of Pisa is a tall marble campanile, which, because of soft ground beneath, is leaning over at an angle.

My Arts List

We covered a lot of ground in this chapter: beautiful art, all types of music, even some stuff about buildings. So this final list covers a lot of ground, too. Write small if you have to.

My favourite style of art to see _____

My favourite style of art to make _____

My favourite painting/sculpture _____

My favourite colour(s) _____

I can play this instrument (if any) _____

I wish I could play this instrument _____

My favourite instrument
to hear played is _____

My favourite style of music is _____

I've seen or heard an opera
(yes or no) _____

The style of my house is _____

My favourite style of building is _____

To make this arts list complete, use the box on the right to draw a self-portrait. Don't worry; you won't be graded on it. Just give it a try. It can't hurt!

CHAPTER EIGHT

Pop Culture

"Pop" means popular, and when you add it to "culture" it means all that stuff you spend your hard-earned allowance on, like movies, books, comics, video games, roller coasters, and other fun stuff.

Best-selling Kids' Books

This list exists thanks to you and to millions of other kids over the past century. It features the top-selling children's books of this century in North America. Your parents may remember many of these fondly, even if you haven't heard of all of them. The best-selling Canadian book on these lists is the popular picture book *Love You Forever* by Robert Munsch.

The Poky Little Puppy	Janette Lowrey, 1942
Charlotte's Web	E. B. White, 1974
The Outsiders	S. E. Hinton, 1968
The Tale of Peter Rabbit	Beatrix Potter, 1902
Tootle	Gertrude Crampton, 1945
Green Eggs and Ham	Dr. Seuss, 1960
Harry Potter and the Philosopher's Stone	J. K. Rowling, 1998
Harry Potter and the Chamber of Secrets	J. K. Rowling, 1999
Harry Potter and the Goblet of Fire	J. K. Rowling, 2000
Tales of a Fourth Grade Nothing	Judy Blume, 1976
Pat the Bunny	Dorothy Kunhardt, 1940
Harry Potter and the Prisoner of Azkaban	J.K. Rowling, 1999
Harry Potter and the Order of the Phoenix	J.K. Rowling, 2003
Love You Forever	Robert Munsch, 1986
Saggy Baggy Elephant	Kathryn and Byron Jackson, 1947
Scuffy the Tugboat	Gertrude Crampton, 1955
The Cat in the Hat	Dr. Seuss, 1957
Where the Red Fern Grows	Wilson Rawls, 1973
Island of the Blue Dolphins	Scott O'Dell, 1971
Are You There, God? It's Me, Margaret	Judy Blume, 1972
Shane	Jack Schaeffer, 1972
The Indian in the Cupboard	Lynne Reid Banks, 1982

J.K. Rowling's Harry Potter books are the only books published since 1990 to break into this list, and it's a sure bet that *Harry Potter and the Half-Blood Prince* will climb the list, too.

Best-selling Comic Books

Holy longevity, Batman! The Caped Crusader first appeared in Detective Comics in 1939. More than 60 years later, in February 2002, he was still atop the list of best-selling comic books.

1. **The Dark Knight Strikes Again #3**
2. **The Ultimates #2**
3. **New X-Men #123**
4. **Uncanny X-Men #403**
5. **Ultimate X-Men #15**
6. **Amazing Spider-Man #40**
7. **Ultimate Spider-Man #19**
8. **Ultimate Spider-Man #18**
9. **X-Treme X-Men #10**
10. **Green Arrow #13**
11. **Wolverine #173**
12. **JLA #63**
13. **Wolverine/Hulk #1**
14. **Avengers #51**
15. **Batman #600**
16. **The Punisher #9**
17. **Peter Parker: Spider-Man #40**
18. **Daredevil #30**
19. **Fantastic Four #52**
20. **X-Force #125**

Superman, who debuted in 1938, was one of the first major national comic-book stars. His popularity helped create the golden age of the superhero in comic books in the 1930s.

Famous Fictional
Places

You can visit the following places, but only in your mind. These locales sprung from the pages of classic books. (Can you name the books or series in which each place originated? Answers are upside down in the right-hand column.)

Camelot
King Arthur legends

Hundred-Acre Wood
Winnie-the-Pooh

Middle Earth
Lord of the Rings

Narnia
Chronicles of Narnia

Neverland
Peter Pan stories

Oz
Wizard of Oz

Gotham City
Batman comic books

Utopia
Utopia

Hogwarts
Harry Potter

Wonderland
Alice's Adventures in Wonderland

The word "utopia," from Sir Thomas More's book about an imaginary island, now means any perfect condition or situation.

Famous Fictional
Characters

Some characters seem real, even if they never existed. Here are some characters who were born from the pens of innovative authors and live on in our imaginations. We're sure you can add your own favourites to the list.

Anne Shirley
Big Bird
Captain Ahab
The Cat in the Hat
Charlotte the Spider
Dracula
Dr. Frankenstein
Dr. Jekyll & Mr. Hyde
Ebenezer Scrooge
Encyclopedia Brown
E.T.
The Grinch
Hamlet

Hardy Boys
Harriet the Spy
Harry Potter
Jacob Two-Two
James Bond
Nancy Drew
Odysseus
Scarlett O'Hara
Sherlock Holmes
Tarzan
Tom Sawyer
Willy Wonka
Winnie-the-Pooh

PsSST "Frankenstein" is the name of the doctor who created the monster in Mary Shelley's classic novel, not the name of the monster itself.

Caldecott Books

Each year since 1938, the Caldecott Medal has been awarded by the Association for Library Service to Children to the most distinguished American picture books for children. Here are recent winners.

2005 *Kitten's First Full Moon* by Kevin Henkes

2004 *The Man Who Walked Between the Towers* by Mordicai Gerstein

2003 *My Friend Rabbit* by Eric Rohmann

2002 *The Three Pigs* by David Wiesner

2001 *So You Want to Be President?*
Illustrated by David Small, text by Judith St. George

2000 *Joseph Had a Little Overcoat* by Simms Taback

1999 *Snowflake Bentley*
Illustrated by Mary Azarian, text by Jacqueline Briggs Martin

1998 *Rapunzel* by Paul O. Zelinsky

1997 *Golem* by David Wisniewski

1996 *Officer Buckle and Gloria* by Peggy Rathmann

1995 *Smoky Night* Illustrated by David Diaz, text by Eve Bunting

1994 *Grandfather's Journey* by Allen Say, text edited by Walter Lorraine

1993 *Mirette on the High Wire* by Emily Arnold McCully

1992 *Tuesday* by David Wiesner

1991 *Black and White* by David Macaulay

1990 *Lon Po Po: A Red-Riding Hood Story from China* by Ed Young

1989 *Song and Dance Man*
Illustrated by Stephen Gammell, text by Karen Ackerman

1988 *Owl Moon* Illustrated by John Schoenherr, text by Jane Yolen

1987 *Hey, Al* Illustrated by Richard Egielski, text by Arthur Yorinks

PsSST

Randolph Caldecott, for whom the medal was named, was a nineteenth-century English illustrator.

Newbery Books

The Newbery Medal annually honours the most distinguished contributions to American literature for children. Here are recent winners.

2005 *Kira-Kira* by Cynthia Kadohata

2004 *The Tale of Despereaux . . .* by Kate DiCamillo

2003 *Crispin: The Cross of Lead* by Avi

2002 *A Single Shard* by Linda Sue Park

2001 *A Year Down Yonder* by Richard Peck

2000 *Bud, Not Buddy* by Christopher Paul Curtis

1999 *Holes* by Louis Sachar

1998 *Out of the Dust* by Karen Hesse

1997 *The View from Saturday* by E.L. Konigsburg

1996 *The Midwife's Apprentice* by Karen Cushman

1995 *Walk Two Moons* by Sharon Creech

1994 *The Giver* by Lois Lowry

1993 *Missing May* by Cynthia Rylant

1992 *Shiloh* by Phyllis Reynolds Naylor

1991 *Maniac Magee* by Jerry Spinelli

1990 *Number the Stars* by Lois Lowry

1989 *Joyful Noise: Poems for Two Voices* by Paul Fleischman

1988 *Lincoln: A Photobiography* by Russell Freedman

1987 *The Whipping Boy* by Sid Fleischman

1986 *Sarah, Plain and Tall* by Patricia MacLachlan

PSSST John Newbery was an eighteenth-century British bookseller. The Newbery Medal was first awarded in 1922.

Great Kids' Books

Beginning in 1975, a new award was created to honour the very best Canadian authors and illustrators of books for children. Honours are given to books in both English and French. Here are lists of recent winners—how many have you read?

Awards for Books in English

YEAR   WINNER FOR WRITING/WINNER FOR ILLUSTRATION

2004 Kenneth Oppel, *Airborn*
       Stéphane Jorisch, *Jabberwocky*

2003 Glen Huser, *Stitches*
       Allen Sapp, *The Song Within My Heart*

2002 Martha Brooks,
       True Confessions of a Heartless Girl
       Wallace Edwards, *Alphabeasts*

2001 Arthur Slade, *Dust*
       Mireille Levert, *An Island in the Soup*

2000 Deborah Ellis, *Looking for X*
       Marie-Louise Gay, *Yuck, a Love Story*

1999 Rachna Gilmore, *A Screaming Kind of Day*
       Gary Clement, *The Great Poochini*

1998 Janet Lunn, *The Hollow Tree*
       Kady MacDonald Denton,
       A Child's Treasury of Nursery Rhymes

1997 Kit Pearson, *Awake and Dreaming*
       Barbara Reid, *The Party*

1996 Paul Yee, *Ghost Train*
       Eric Beddows, *The Rooster's Gift*

1995 Tim Wynne-Jones, *The Maestro*
       Ludmila Zeman, *The Last Quest of Gilgamesh*

Awards for Books in French

YEAR	WINNER FOR WRITING/WINNER FOR ILLUSTRATION
2004	Nicole Leroux, *L'Hiver de Léo Polatouche* Janice Nadeau, *Nul poisson ou aller*
2003	Danielle Simard, *J'ai vendu ma soeur* Virginie Egger, *Recette d'éléphant a la sauce vieux*
2002	Hélène Vachon, *L'oiseau de passage* Luc Melanson, *Le grand voyage de Monsieur*
2001	Christiane Duchesne, *Jomusch et le troll des cuisines* Bruce Roberts, *Fidéles éléphants*
2000	Charlotte Gingras, *Un été de Jade* Anne Villeneuvè, *L'Écharpe rouge*
1999	Charlotte Gingras, *La Liberté? Connais pas . . .* Stéphane Jorisch, *Charlotte et l'île du destin*
1998	Angèle Delaunois, *Variations sur un même «t'aime»* Pierre Pratt, *Monsieur Ilétaitunefois*
1997	Michel Noël, *Pien* Stéphane Poulin, *Poil de serpent, dent d'araignée*
1996	Gilles Tibo, *Noémie: Le Secret de Madame Lumbago* No award
1995	Sonia Sarfati, *Comme une peau de chagrin* Annouchka G. Galouchko, *Sho et les dragons d'eau*

PsSST These Governor General's Literary Awards are given out each year by the Canada Council for the Arts. The Council also rewards authors of works for adults in fiction, poetry, drama, nonfiction, and translation.

Best-selling Musicians

According to the Recording Industry Association of America, these are the best-selling recording artists of all time. Are your favourites on the list?

1. Elvis Presley
2. Garth Brooks
3. Billy Joel
4. Barbra Streisand
5. Elton John
6. Bruce Springsteen
7. Madonna
8. Michael Jackson
9. Mariah Carey
10. George Strait
11. Whitney Houston
12. Kenny Rogers
13. Neil Diamond
14. Kenny G
15. Céline Dion
16. Shania Twain
17. Willie Nelson
18. Eric Clapton
19. 2Pac
20. Prince

Michael Jackson's *Thriller* (1982) has sold more copies than any other album released by an individual. The overall record is held by the Eagles, whose *Greatest Hits: 1971-75* has sold more than 27 million copies, just ahead of *Thriller*'s 26 million.

Best-selling Groups

The Beatles are history's best-selling group, according to the Recording Industry Association of America—and it's not even a close race. The Fab Four's sales are more than 50 percent better than runner-up Led Zeppelin. Here are the top 20 groups.

1. The Beatles
2. Led Zeppelin
3. Eagles
4. Pink Floyd
5. Aerosmith
6. The Rolling Stones
7. AC/DC
8. Metallica
9. Van Halen
10. Fleetwood Mac
11. U2
12. Alabama
13. Santana
14. Journey
15. Simon and Garfunkel
16. Chicago
17. Silver Bullet Band
18. Foreigner
19. Guns 'n' Roses
20. Backstreet Boys

The Beatles remain popular more than three decades after their last concert. *1*, a collection of their number-one singles, was released in 2000 and immediately soared to the top of the album charts.

Grammy Winners

Sir Georg Solti is an internationally renowned conductor who has led the Chicago Symphony Orchestra and the London Philharmonic, among others. Never heard of him? That's okay, he's never heard of you. Here's the list of everyone who's won a dozen or more of the coveted Grammy awards, which are named after the gramaphone, the first version of the record player. (Ask your mom what a "record" was . . . She will probably sigh.)

ARTIST	AWARDS	ARTIST	AWARDS
Sir Georg Solti	30	Itzhak Perlman	14
Quincy Jones	26	Ella Fitzgerald	13
Vladimir Horowitz	25	Leontyne Price	13
Henry Mancini	20	Robert Shaw	13
Stevie Wonder	17	Chet Atkins	12
Leonard Bernstein	16	Ray Charles	12
Paul Simon	16	David Foster	12
Aretha Franklin	15	Michael Jackson	12
John Williams	15	Thomas Z. Shepard	12
Pierre Boulez	14	Sting	12

What do Elvis Presley, the Beatles, Bing Crosby, the Rolling Stones, and Boyz II Men have in common? None of those successful performers ever earned a Grammy for Record of the Year. Paul Simon, on the other hand, has won the award an all-time best three times.

So Young...
So Talented

And the winner is . . . not even a teenager yet. Anna Paquin was only 11 years old when she won an Oscar in 1993 as Best Supporting Actress for her role in *The Piano*. But Paquin wasn't the youngest recipient ever in that category. Here are the youngest winners in some of the Academy Awards' key categories.

AGE   WINNER
CATEGORY/MOTION PICTURE/YEAR

29 Adrien Brody
Best Actor, *The Pianist*, 2002

21 Marlee Matlin
Best Actress, *Children of a Lesser God*, 1986

20 Timothy Hutton
Best Supporting Actor, *Ordinary People*, 1980

11 Anna Paquin
Best Supporting Actress, *The Piano*, 1993

10 Tatum O'Neal
Best Supporting Actress, *Paper Moon*, 1973

PsSST

Several youngsters have earned honourary awards for their work in movies. The youngest was six-year-old Shirley Temple in 1935. The award: a miniature Oscar statuette!

Rated L for Lists

Wonder why Mom and Dad don't want you to see that scary/bloody/violent/cool movie playing at the mall? They've considered the ratings. Canada's provinces and territories set their own ratings, and there are some differences from place to place. Here is a summary of the ratings:

G   General Audiences—All Ages Admitted.

Suitable for viewing by all ages.

PG   Parental Guidance.

Parents should decide if they want their children to see the film, which may contain adult themes, some profanity, violence, or brief nudity.

14A 14 Accompaniment.

People under 14 years of age must be accompanied by an adult. The film might contain violence, "coarse" language, or adult themes.

18A 18 Accompaniment.

People under 18 years of age must be accompanied by an adult. The film will likely have a lot of violence, adult themes, horror, or "coarse" language.

Restricted No One Under 18 Admitted.

The film contains elements that most parents would consider off-limits for viewing by their children.

The system in Quebec differs the most from those in other provinces. There the levels are G (all ages); 13+ (13 and older); 16+ (16 and older); and 18+ (18 and older).

Biggest Movies

These flicks have big B.O.! No, they don't stink . . . in fact, just the opposite. These movies have taken in more money at the box office ("b.o." — get it?) than any others. Of course, this list is always changing as Hollywood creates more amazing movies. How many on this list have you seen? Note: This list includes movies released in the United States and Canada through the middle of 2005, and it doesn't include video or DVD sales!

MOVIE (YEAR)	MILLIONS CAN$
Titanic (1997)	**$723.9**
Star Wars (1977)	**$555.4**
Shrek 2 (2004)	**$526.7**
E.T.: The Extra-Terrestrial (1982)	**$524.1**
Star Wars: The Phantom Menace (1999)	**$519.5**
Spider-Man: The Movie (2002)	**$486.6**
Lord of the Rings: The Return of the King (2003)	**$455.1**
Spider-Man 2 (2004)	**$449.9**
The Passion of the Christ (2004)	**$446.2**
Jurassic Park (1993)	**$430.4**

Movie studios compete for having the biggest "opening" of their movies. That means how much money a movie makes in its first day, its first weekend, or its first week. A movie that opens big often can turn into a mega-blockbuster, while a movie that doesn't open well can turn into a flop.

Very Rich Cartoons

Shrek 2 blew away the competition (we won't say how . . .) to become not only the most successful animated film ever, but also among the all-time top ten box-office hits in motion-picture history. Guess the other films are the ones that are, um, green. Here are the top ten money-making full-length animated movies. How many have you seen?

1. Shrek 2

2. Finding Nemo

3. The Lion King

4. Shrek

5. The Incredibles

6. Monsters, Inc.

7. Toy Story 2

8. Aladdin

9. Toy Story

10. Snow White and the Seven Dwarfs

The original *Toy Story*, which was released in 1995, was the first full-length film to be completely created using computer animation.

Cartoon Families

Although sometimes it seems as if your family is a cartoon, it's not on this list. This list includes the members of some of the most well-known families in cartoons and comics. We left a line at the end to include your favourites, in case they didn't make our list.

CARTOON CHARACTERS/
KEY FAMILY MEMBERS

Arthur the Aardvark
Dad, Mom, Arthur, D.W., Kate

Babar
King Babar, Queen Celeste, Flora, Pom, Isabelle, Alexander, cousin Arthur

The Ducks
Donald and his nephews Huey, Dewey, and Louie

The Flintstones and Rubbles
Fred, Wilma, and Pebbles; Barney, Betty, and Bam-Bam

Franklin
Mom, Dad, Franklin, Harriet, and Goldie

The Jetsons
George, Jane, Judy, and Elroy

CARTOON CHARACTERS/
KEY FAMILY MEMBERS

The Powerpuffs
Bubbles, Blossom, and Buttercup

The Pickles (from Rugrats)
Stu, Didi, Grandpa Lou, Tommy, and Dylan, plus Grandma Minka and Grandpa Boris, Uncle Drew, and cousin Angelica

Rolie Polie Olie
Mom, Dad, Olie, and Zowie

The Simpsons
Homer, Marge, Bart, Lisa, and Maggie

_____

_____

The Simpsons **characters originally appeared in short films on** *The Tracey Ullman Show.* **Creator Matt Groening supposedly made them up while waiting to go into a meeting with that show's producers. The shorts were so popular that** *The Simpsons* **got their own half-hour show in 1989.**

Who Owns TVs?

There are more than four television sets for every five people in the United States, the highest ratio in the world. How many do you have? How many do you wish you had? These countries have the most TV sets.

COUNTRY	SETS PER 1,000 PEOPLE
United States	806
Canada	710
Japan	686
Finland	622
France	595
Denmark	594
Germany	567
Australia	554
Czech Republic	531
Italy	528

A 2004 study found that Canadians watch an average of 21.6 hours of TV per week. At more than 24 hours per week, French-speaking folks in Quebec watched the most.

Canadian Surfers!

By March, 2005 about 20,400,000, or about 64 percent, of Canadians were using the Internet, and spending more than 34 hours a month online. That's some serious Web surfing. Here are some more interesting Internet statistics for the year 2004, according to a Yahoo! Canada survey.

Canadian Internet users were almost equal according to gender—49.2 percent female and 50.8 percent male.

Users spent about 84 minutes online each day they surfed the Web.

About 48 percent of users said they couldn't go without the Internet for more than two weeks.

In November, 2004 more than 15.5 million Canadians went shopping online.

By the end of 2004, Canadians were receiving an average of 177 e-mails a week.

Almost 50 percent of those e-mails were spam— unwanted junk mail.

Nearly 23 percent of all spam worldwide originated in the United States.

Canada was number ten on the source-of-spam list, generating 2 percent of the world's spam.

The pop singer Canadian surfers looked for most often on the web in 2004 was Avril Lavigne.

The top six items Canadian and American on-line shoppers were checking out in 2004 were: Playstation 2, digital cameras, toys, sporting goods, Nintendo DS, and books.

Your Parents'
Favourite Shows

You know your favourite shows to watch on TV. But what did your parents watch when they were younger? Here are some shows that were popular more than 20 years ago. Ask an older family member about these and watch them get all misty-eyed and nostalgic.

The Beachcombers

The Brady Bunch

Captain Kangaroo

Cosby Show

The Edison Twins

The Electric Company

Fat Albert and the Cosby Kids

Flipper

Happy Days

H.R. Pufnstuf

Laverne & Shirley

Lost in Space

Mork & Mindy

Mister Rogers' Neighborhood*

Mr. Dressup*

Sesame Street*

* These are shows that both you and your parents probably watched!

Ernie Coombs, better known as "Mr. Dressup," was a television icon beloved by Canadian children for decades. His show was on TV from 1967 to 1996.

Kids on TV

You love to watch yourself on TV. That is, you love to watch kids on TV. There have been kid stars on TV from Jerry Mathers on *Leave It to Beaver* to Mary-Kate and Ashley Olsen on *Full House*. Here are a few top kid stars from yesterday and today, and the shows they appeared or appear on.

YESTERDAY

STAR	TV SHOW
Melissa Sue Anderson	*Little House on the Prairie*
Tempestt Bledsoe	*The Cosby Show*
Soleil Moon Frye	*Punky Brewster*
Melissa Gilbert	*Little House on the Prairie*
Ron Howard	*The Andy Griffith Show*
Jay North	*Dennis the Menace*
Butch Patrick	*The Munsters*
Jonathan Taylor Thomas	*Home Improvement*

TODAY

Hilary Duff	*Lizzie McGuire*
David Gallagher	*7th Heaven*
Miriam McDonald	*Degrassi: The Next Generation*
Frankie Muniz	*Malcolm in the Middle*
Raven	*That's So Raven*
Jamie Lynn Spears	*All That/Zoey 101*
Ricky Ullman	*Phil of the Future*
Camille Winbush	*The Bernie Mac Show*

Frankie Muniz was nominated for an Emmy as best actor in a comedy in 2001, but at 11 years old, he wasn't the youngest nominee ever. In 1990, Fred Savage of *The Wonder Years* was a few months younger than Frankie when he was nominated. He didn't win, either!

Computer and Video Games

Face it — if you're a kid, somewhere along the line you're going to play and/or own a computer game or a video game of some sort. You're not alone. Here are some of the most popular video games (as of mid-2005) for a variety of platforms.

Sony Playstation 2

Grand Theft Auto: San Andreas
God of War
NCAA Football 06
Killer7
Gran Turismo 4

Nintendo GameCube

Killer7
Resident Evil 4
Mario Power Tennis
Super Smash Brothers Melee

Microsoft XBox

Halo 2
NCAA Football 06
Tom Clancy's Ghost Recon 2: Summit Strike
Grand Theft Auto: San Andreas
Sid Meier's Pirates!
Destroy All Humans!

Sony Playstation Portable

Coded Arms
Dead to Rights: Reckoning
Final Fantasy VII: Advent Children
Midnight Club 3

Computer Games for PC

Battlefield 2
Half-Life 2
Grand Theft Auto: San Andreas
Roller Coaster Tycoon 3
The Sims 2
World of Warcraft

Nintendo GameBoy Advance

Riviera: The Promised Land
Pokemon Emerald
Fantastic 4

You probably know this already, but most game makers insert secret points or parts of the game called "Easter eggs." Players need to know secret codes or combinations of keys to make the "eggs" appear.

Hall of Fame Games

Games magazine is the top publication for people who love games of all sorts: word games, math games, board games, picture games, etc. The editors of the magazine have created the "Games Hall of Fame" to honour board games that are popular favourites. Here is their list of the greatest games. We can't believe they didn't include Candyland!

Acquire

Axis and Allies

Blockhead!

Bridgette

Clue

Civilization

Diplomacy

Dungeons and Dragons

Mille Bornes

Monopoly

Othello

Pente

Risk

Scrabble

Sorry!

Stratego

Taboo

TriBond

Trivial Pursuit

Twister

Twixt

Yahtzee

Monopoly is the best-selling board game of all time, with more than 200 million copies sold since it was first produced in 1935. There are now versions for cities, countries, colleges, and sports teams, as well as editions in 26 languages. The street names in the original game are all named after streets found in Atlantic City, New Jersey.

Popular Card Games

It's raining. You're on a long car trip. The cable's out again. What're you gonna do? Why not play a nice game of cards? Here's a list of some of the most popular card games, a few of which have been around for centuries. Your family probably has a favourite. Good luck!

Authors	**Go Fish!**
Blackjack	**Hearts**
Bridge	**Old Maid**
Canasta	**Pinochle**
Concentration	**Poker**
Cribbage	**Solitaire**
Crazy Eights	**Uno**
Euchre	**War**

The joker playing card was introduced to American card decks in the 1860s. In the game of Euchre, players wanted an extra "trump" card (a card that beats other cards). Card makers added the joker to the "royal court" of king, queen, and jack.

Famous Cowpeople

The cowboy image we have from Hollywood comes from seeing the likes of John Wayne and Kirk Douglas on the big screen. The cowgirl image started out as pretty frilly, but it's gotten rougher and tougher (and more real). Here are some famous people who made their living on the ranches or frontiers of the Old West and not necessarily on the screen.

COWBOYS

Jesse Chisholm
John Chisum
Charles Goodnight
John Wesley Iliff
Richard King
Oliver Loving
John Lytle
Samuel Maverick
Joseph McCoy
Nelson Story
Alexander Swan
Andrew Voigt

COWGIRLS

Calamity Jane
(Martha Jane Canary)
Mary Ann Goodnight
Charmayne James
Henrietta King
Florence LaDue
Goldia Bays Malone
Lucille Mulhall
Annie Oakley
Narcissa Prentiss Whitman
Lizzie Williams

Ya say ya ain't heard 'bout lotta these cowfolks? Well, check out the Cowboy Hall of Fame on that newfangled Internet!

"Cowgirl" was first used to describe Lucille Mulhall in the early 1900s, and the name stuck. Various reports credit Theodore Roosevelt or Will Rogers with coining the term.

Biggest Amusement Parks

Disney parks are the most popular parks in the world. Here are the most frequented parks around the globe in 2004.

AMUSEMENT PARK	LOCATION
The Magic Kingdom at Walt Disney World	Florida
Disneyland	California
Tokyo Disneyland	Japan
Tokyo Disney Sea	Japan
Disneyland Paris	France
Universal Studios	Japan
Epcot at Walt Disney World	Florida
Disney-MGM Studios at Walt Disney World	Florida
Lotte World	South Korea
Disney's Animal Kingdom at Walt Disney World	Florida
Blackpool Pleasure Beach	England
Universal Studios	Florida
Universal's Islands of Adventure	Florida
Yokohama Hakkeijima Sea Paradise	Japan
Disney's California Adventures	California
Universal Studios Hollywood	California
Seaworld Florida	Florida
Nagashima Spa Land	Japan
Tivoli Gardens	Denmark

The oldest amusement park in the world is Bakken, which is near Copenhagen, Denmark. It first opened in 1583. We hope they've cleaned out the popcorn machine a few times since then.

Fastest Roller Coasters

Roller-coaster enthusiasts yearn for either wooden or steel roller coasters. Both sides claim that their type of roller coaster offers the most thrills. In the end, however, the biggest thrill may be the speed.

KM/MILES PER HOUR	ROLLER COASTER/LOCATION
206/128	**Kingda**/Six Flags Great Adventure, New Jersey
193/120	**Top Thrill Dragster**/Cedar Point, Ohio
171/106	**Dodonpa**/Fujikyu Highland, Japan
161/100	**Superman-The Escape** Six Flags Magic Mountain, California
161/100	**Tower of Terror**/Dreamworld, Australia
152/95	**Steel Dragon 2000**/Nagashima Spa Land, Japan
150/93	**Millennium Force**/Cedar Point, Ohio
137/85	**Goliath**/Six Flags Magic Mountain, California
137/85	**Titan**/Six Flags Over Texas, Texas
132/82	**Phantom's Revenge**/Pennsylvania*
132/82	**Xcelerator**/Knott's Berry Farm, California
130/80.8	**Fujiyama**/Fujikyu Highland, Japan
129/80	**Desperado**/Buffalo Bill's Resort/Casino, Nevada
129/80	**HyperSonic XLC**/King Dominion, Virginia

* Kennywood Park, Pennsylvania

PsSST Steel roller coasters top the list for those thrill seekers wanting speed. Son of Beast, at Paramount's King Island, Ohio, is the fastest wood roller coaster at **126 kph (78.4 mph)**.

Fabulous Fads

A "fad" is something that millions of people suddenly seem to be doing, wearing, or eating all at once — and then it's gone almost as quickly as it appeared. Fads can be clothes, dances, music, toys, activities, or just about anything. Here are some of North America's wildest, weirdest, and most popular fads. The years listed are the height of the fad's popularity.

1920s   Raccoon coats
College kids wore enormous overcoats made of raccoon skins.

1924   Flagpole sitting
People tried to see how long they could stay atop a flagpole.

1939   Goldfish swallowing
. . . and we don't mean crackers! Don't try this at home.

1950s   Bomb shelters
People afraid of atomic bombs built underground rooms in their backyards; they thought they would be safe there during an attack.

1950s   Poodle skirts
Long, wide, colourful skirts with big appliqués of poodles on them.

1955   Coonskin caps
Kids everywhere wore these caps, modelled after the ones worn on the TV show *Davy Crockett.*

1959   Phone booth stuffing
How many bored college kids can you squeeze into a phone booth? They also tried this with Volkswagen Beetles.

1960s   Tie-dyed T-shirts
A totally groovy fashion made by tying shirts into knots and then dying them, usually purple.

1962   Alvin and the Chipmunks
These squeaky-voiced cartoon "singers" were a huge hit for years. They were actually people's singing voices speeded up.

1970s   Platform shoes
How high can you go? Platform shoes made girls stand out in the 1970s. This is one fad that has made a recent comeback.

1973   Puka shells
Little white seashells worn on chokers by both boys and girls.

1974   Streaking
Running through public places with no clothes on. Really.

1975   CB radios
CB stands for "citizens' band," a type of radio first used by truckers. A song made them popular with many other people — but only for a while, good buddy. 10-4!

1975   Pet Rocks
Believe it or not, millions of people paid good money for a box with a rock in it. That was it, a rock that people kept for a pet.

1980   Rubik's Cube
This extremely difficult multicoloured puzzle was a rage for years; you can still find them in some people's toy closets.

1982   Smurfs
They were blue, they had a funny language, and they were everywhere! Smurfs were cartoon characters from Belgium.

1983   Cabbage Patch Kids
If you didn't have one of these dolls (which were so popular for a while that they were hard to get), you just weren't "in."

1989   Teenage Mutant Ninja Turtles
Four turtles who knew karate, talked like surfers, and lived in the sewer. North America couldn't get enough of them.

1993   Macarena
You might have heard the song or done the dance, which was everywhere for about a year, but then vanished just as quickly.

1994   POGs
These were collectible cardboard disks, first created in Hawaii, that were pretty much the next Pet Rocks — hugely popular, then gone. POG stood for passion-orange-guava juice. The disks were originally inside bottle caps of that drink.

What fads are coming next? Kids in North America should look to the West. Many of today's fashion, video-game, and music fads are coming from Japan. They usually hit North America's west coast first.

Black Cats and Rabbits' Feet

See a penny, pick it up, all the day you'll have good luck. Most of us learned that one a long time ago. Here are some other common signs that things are going to go your way. The other list is one of bad luck signs.

GOOD LUCK

A four-leaf clover

A cricket inside the house

A horseshoe hung above the doorway

A rabbit's foot

A rainbow

Eating black-eyed peas on New Year's Day

Crossed fingers

Carrying the bride over the threshold

Keeping a chain letter going

When the first butterfly you see in a new year is white

Finding a penny that is facing heads-up

BAD LUCK

A black cat crossing your path

Walking under a ladder

The number 13 (especially Friday the thirteenth)

Breaking a mirror

Opening an umbrella inside the house

Stepping on cracks

Spilling salt (unless you throw a pinch over your left shoulder)

Killing a ladybug

Placing a hat on a bed

A groom seeing his bride before the ceremony on the wedding day

Seeing three butterflies together

Breaking a chain letter

When you hang that horseshoe above the doorway, be sure to keep the open end up. Otherwise, all the good luck will fall out!

Are You Listaphobic?

The word "phobia" is used to describe a condition in which a person is very, very scared of something. There are lots of things to be scared of, and there's a phobia for just about all of them. For instance, are you afraid of spiders? If so, you're not alone. In fact, fear of spiders (arachnophobia) is the most common phobia. Here are some of the fears with the most fearers, er, people.

Spiders	Arachnophobia
People and social situations	Anthrophobia
Flying	Aerophobia
Open spaces	Agoraphobia
Confined spaces	Claustrophobia
Vomiting	Emetophobia
Heights	Acrophobia
Cancer	Carcinomaphobia
Thunderstorms	Brontophobia
Death	Necrophobia
Heart Disease	Cardiophobia

So many folks associate the number 13 with bad luck (see the signs of good luck and bad luck on the opposite page) that there's a word for their fear: triskaidekaphobia.

My Favourites

This chapter is full of top singers, movies, TV shows, and more. But what are your favourites? Here's a page for you to make your own top ten lists.

MY FAVOURITE TV SHOWS

1._____   6._____

2._____   7._____

3._____   8._____

4._____   9._____

5._____   10._____

MY FAVOURITE MOVIES

1._____   6._____

2._____   7._____

3._____   8._____

4._____   9._____

5._____   10._____

MY FAVOURITE SINGERS OR GROUPS

1._____   6._____

2._____   7._____

3._____   8._____

4._____   9._____

5._____   10._____

CHAPTER NINE

Critters

Lions and tigers and bears . . . and dogs and cats and egg–laying mammals and flying monkeys and an exaltation of larks. Plus a horse named Ed and a cow that says "mu."

Endangered Animals

An animal species is endangered if its ability to survive is threatened. The reasons for this include disease, destruction of its habitat (where they live), too much hunting, or overfishing. Here are some animals from around the world that are officially recognized as endangered.

Asian elephant
Bison
Blue whale
California condor
Cheetah
Chimpanzee
Florida manatee
Flying squirrel
Giant armadillo
Giant panda
Gorilla
Jaguar
Komodo dragon
Lemur
Leopard
Marine otter
Ocelot
Orangutan
Tiger
Whooping crane

In 1944, there were only 21 whooping cranes left in the world. Thanks to the efforts of a group of Canadian and American scientists, there are now more than 400!

Extinct Animals

Extinct means you won't be seeing any of these animals at the zoo anytime soon — or anywhere else for that matter. Some of these animals died out naturally; others were simply hunted by humans into extinction. Dinosaurs have been extinct for millions of years, though it's open to debate exactly what caused their demise. Here are some examples of other animals that ceased to exist a bit more recently.

ANIMAL	LAST ALIVE
Balinese tiger	1937
Blue pike	1970
Caribbean monk seal	1922
Dodo bird	1681
Great auk	1844
Heath hen	1932
Passenger pigeon	1914
Sabre-toothed tiger	c. 9000 B.C.
Stellar's sea cow	1768
Tasmanian tiger-wolf	1936
Woolly mammoth	c. 2000 B.C.
Woolly rhinoceros	c. 8000 B.C.

The Tasmanian tiger-wolf was neither a tiger nor a wolf. In fact, it was a marsupial that had a front pouch for its young, much like a kangaroo.

Deeeeep Sleepers

How would you like to go to bed in November and wake up in March? Well, you'd miss out on New Year's, so maybe it wouldn't be that cool. However, some animals do sleep that long. Everyone knows about bears that "hibernate" in the winter, but here are some other animals that get some Big Sleep.

Bat
Box Turtle
Eastern Chipmunk
Ground Squirrel
Jumping Mouse
Raccoon
Skunk
Snake
Toad
Woodchuck

PsSST

Hibernation means much more than sleeping soundly. An animal's bodily functions almost come to a halt. Breathing rate and pulse slow down a lot, and body temperature may drop.

Get Me Out of Here!

That's what the babies of the animals in this list are saying. The word "gestation" means how long an animal is inside its mother before being born. Some animals really like to hold onto their babies and have very long gestation periods. These animals carry babies for the longest times.

ANIMAL	GESTATION PERIOD (IN DAYS)
Elephant	510–730
Whale	365–547
Donkey	about 365
Horse	329–345
Deer	197–300
Cow	about 280
Monkey	139–270
Hippopotamus	220–255
Bear	180–240
Goat	136–160
Sheep	144–152
Pig	101–130
Lion	105–113

For human beings, pregnancy generally is considered nine months. Technically, it's anywhere from 253 to 303 days.

Do German

Cows say "moo" all over the world, right? Well, yes and no. The sounds an animal makes are the same, but they are expressed differently in different

ANIMAL	ENGLISH	RUSSIAN
Bird	Tweet-tweet	Squick
Cat	Meow	Meau
Cow	Moo	Mu
Dog	Bow-wow	Guf-guf
Duck	Quack-quack	Quack
Goat	Meh-meh	Beee
Horse	Neigh-neigh	Eohoho
Owl	Whoo	Ooooo
Pig	Oink-oink	Qrr-qrrr
Rooster	Cock-a-doodle-do	Kukuriki

When does a frog sound like a duck? When it's German, of course. In English, a frog says "ribbit." But in German, it comes out "quaak, quaak."

Cows Moo?

languages. Here are some common animal sounds and how they are expressed in five languages.

JAPANESE	FRENCH	GERMAN
Qui-qui	Choon-choon	Piep-piep
Nyeow	Meow	Meow-meow
Mo-Mo	Meu-meu	Muh-muh
Won-won	Whou-whou	Vow-vow
Qua-qua	Coin-coin	Quack
Mee-mee	Ma-ma	Eeh-eeh
He-heeh	Hee-hee-hee	Iiiih
Hoo-hoo	Oo-oo	Wooo-wooo
Boo	Groan-groan	Crr-cvl
KoKeKock-ko	Cocorico	Goockle

What is the loudest land mammal? Hint: Look up when you're in the jungle.

The howler monkey's shriek can be heard five kilometres (three miles) away!

Pigs (etc.) in Space

The first animal in space was a female mixed-breed dog named Laika, who was aboard the Soviet Union's *Sputnik II* in 1957. Tossing your cat in the air does not qualify it for this list of animals that have travelled in space.

Beetles	**Monkeys**
Bullfrogs	**Rats**
Chimpanzees	**Snails**
Fruit flies	**Swordtail fish**
Medaka fish	**Wasps**
Mice	

BONUS BIT! Miss Baker was the name of a long-tailed squirrel monkey sent to space aboard a U.S. missile in 1959. Despite travelling at more than 16,000 km (10,000 miles) per hour to an altitude of 480 km (300 miles), tiny Miss Baker had little trouble with liftoff, reentry, or weightlessness, which were important test results for manned flight. But the trek did make her a bit cranky. After the flight, she bit the person who removed her from the capsule!

PsSST Laika had a special doggy-shaped space suit made for her. It was made so her four legs stuck out of the suit, perhaps to make it easier for her to go for a "space walk."

Animals in History

One of the most famous animals in history is not a real animal at all. English author A. A. Milne's fictional character of Winnie-the-Pooh is beloved by children around the world. But Winnie was named after a real black bear in the London Zoo. A Canadian soldier had brought the bear from Canada, and called it Winnie after his hometown of Winnipeg.

Balto The Siberian husky that was the lead dog on a lengthy Alaskan trek to deliver lifesaving medicine in 1925.

Big Ben Champion Grand Prix jumping horse from Canada.

Chips German shepherd–collie–husky that was awarded a Purple Heart in World War II.

Koko Gorilla trained to use American Sign Language.

Laika Dog that was the first animal in space in 1957.

Mrs. O'Leary's Cow Sometimes called Daisy, Madeline, or Gwendolyn, she was the cow that allegedly kicked over a lantern that started the Great Chicago Fire of 1871.

Pat Prime Minister William Lyon Mackenzie King's beloved Irish terrier. When Pat died in 1941, Canada went into mourning. Some people say that Pat was better liked than his master!

Wiarton Willie Albino groundhog in Wiarton, Ontario, who predicts the weather on Groundhog Day.

Seabiscuit The legendary racehorse who, according to his recent biography, was the biggest newsmaker of 1938 — bigger even than Franklin Roosevelt or Adolf Hitler.

PsSST Balto's heroic journey to deliver medicine to children in a remote Alaskan village inspired the Iditarod, the annual dog-sled race from Nome to Anchorage.

Not Just Us Chickens

Chickens lay most of the eggs that we eat. (What's your favourite? Scrambled, boiled, fried . . . salad?) All birds, in fact, lay eggs. But birds aren't the only animals that lay eggs. Here are a few more that do.

Butterfly

Crocodile

Duckbill Platypus

Echidna
(Spiny Anteater)

Fish

Frog

Ladybug

Snake

Toad

Turtle

Animals that lay eggs are called "oviparous." Animals that give birth to live offspring from the mother's body are called "viviparous."

Dogs and Cats Living Together

Polar bears eat too much, and beavers just chew up the furniture. So dogs and cats are instead the most popular pets in Canada. Listed here, from most popular to least popular, are the top breeds of cats and dogs in the country, according to national dog and cat organizations.

DOGS	CATS
Labrador Retriever	Persian
Golden Retriever	Maine Coon
German Shepherd	Siamese
Poodle	Exotic shorthair
Shetland Sheepdog	Abyssinian
Miniature Schnauzer	Oriental shorthair
Yorkshire Terrier	American shorthair
Beagle	Scottish fold
Bichon Frise	Burmese
Shih Tzu	Cornish rex
Boxer	Birman
Bernese Mountain Dog	Tonkinese
Pomeranian	
Soft-Coated Wheaten Terrier	

A dog is listed in the *Guinness Book of World Records* for something that's truly mouth-watering: *his* mouth, that is. His tongue is 33 cm (15 inches) long. It's almost always lolling out of his mouth like a red, wet snake!

Animal Group Names

Smack, prickle, and gulp. No, that's not the name of a new breakfast cereal. Those are words called "collective" nouns. Collective nouns are special words that describe a particular group of things — in this case, animals.

A **shrewdness** of apes

A **colony** of bats

A **wake** of buzzards

A **bed** of clams

A **gulp** of cormorants

A **bask** of crocodiles

A **murder** of crows

A **brace** of ducks

A **convocation** of eagles

A **business** of ferrets

A **stand** of flamingos

A **hatch** of flies

A **tower** of giraffes

A **band** of gorillas

An **army** of herring

A **bloat** of hippopotamuses

A **passel** of hogs

A **cackle** of hyenas

A **smack** of jellyfish

A **troop** of kangaroos

An **exaltation** of larks

A **pride** of lions

A **plague** of locusts

A **richness** of martens

A **labour** of moles

A **romp** of otters

A **parliament** of owls

A **muster** of peacocks

A **prickle** of porcupines

A **covey** of quail

A **warren** of rabbits

An **unkindness** of ravens

A **crash** of rhinoceroses

A **pod** of seals (or whales)

A **shiver** of sharks

A **nest** of snakes

A **murmuration** of starlings

A **streak** of tigers

A **knot** of toads

A **gang** of turkeys

See if you can make up some collective nouns for your school or friends. Your class can become a "power" of kids and your neighbours can be a "pile" of people. Have fun with it!

Baby Animal Names

Some baby animal names are well known, like a bear cub or puppy dog. But did you know that a baby skunk is called a kitten or that a baby turtle is called a chicken? Here are some other baby names for animals, including the obvious and the not-so-obvious.

ANIMAL	BABY	ANIMAL	BABY
Ant	antling	Kangaroo	joey
Canary	chick	Lion	shelp, cub, or lionet
Cat	kit, kitling, kitten, or pussy	Ostrich	chick
Chicken	chick, chicken, poult, cockerel, or pullet	Owl	owlet or howlet
Chimpanzee	infant	Penguin	fledgling or chick
Cow	calf	Possum	joey
Duck	duckling or flapper	Rabbit	kit
Eagle	eaglet	Raccoon	kit or cub
Elephant	calf	Rhinoceros	calf
Fish	fry, fingerling, minnow, or spawn	Seal	whelp, pup, cub, or bachelor
Fly	grub or maggot	Shark	cub
Frog	polliwog or tadpole	Sheep	lamb, lambkin, or shearling
Giraffe	calf	Squirrel	dray
Goat	kid	Swan	cygnet
Goose	gosling	Tiger	whelp or cub
Horse	colt, foal, stat, stag, filly, youngster, yearling, or hogget	Toad	tadpole
		Whale	calf
		Zebra	colt or foal

PsSST

A father Emperor penguin protects the penguin mother's egg or eggs for 60 days, standing on his feet the whole time. He doesn't eat while waiting for the chicks to hatch, and he can lose up to 12 kg (26.4 lb.).

FAST-MOVING FISH

Most folks know that the cheetah is the fastest animal on land. Those fast cats can cruise along at up to 113 km (70 miles) per hour. The peregrine falcon is the fastest animal in the air, whipping along at speeds above 160 km (100 miles) per hour. But what about fish? What animals move through the water with the greatest of speed? Go ahead, try to catch them!

FISH	KILOMETRES PER HOUR	MILES PER HOUR
Sailfish	109.8	68.2
Mako shark	96	60
Marlin	80	50
Wahoo	78	48.5
Bluefin tuna	69.8	43.4
Blue shark	69	43
Bonefish	64	40
Swordfish	64	40

PSSST On the other end of the scale, the sea horse won't be winning any underwater races. This very patient little animal has been clocked at .016 km (0.01 miles) per hour.

Bizarre Insect Facts

We're totally outnumbered here — we humans, that is. There are more than 1.25 million species of animals in the world (including us), and 80 percent of those species — more than 1 million — are insects! We're surrounded! Here are a few fascinating facts about insects.

BIGGEST

Several varieties of beetle compete for the title of biggest insect. South America's Acteon beetle is the bulkiest at 8.9 cm (3½ inches) long, 5 cm (2 inches) wide, and 3.8 cm (1½ inches) thick. The goliath, rhinoceros, and longhorned beetles can grow to as much as 12.7 to 17.7 cm (5 to 7 inches) long. But the heaviest insect on record is the giant weta, which once was documented at 142 grams (5 ounces); some insects weigh 1/100th of that!

LONGEST

Stick insects can grow to 35.5 cm (14 inches) long!

SMALLEST

The feather-winged beetle and the fairy fly check in at just .25 mm (1/100th of an inch) long.

FASTEST FLYER

The tabanid fly has been timed flying at 144 kph (90 mph).

FASTEST RUNNER

The cockroach can reach speeds in excess of 1.61 kph (1 mph), which is fast for an insect, trust us.

MOST

Beetles not only are among the largest insects, but they make up the largest group of insects. There are more than half a million species of beetles categorized into 125 different families.

The female praying mantis is perhaps the cruellest insect. It's not unusual for them to bite off the heads of male praying mantises or to eat their own young. Yuck!

A Lot of Candles

The box turtle doesn't move very fast, but maybe that's because it's got lots of time on its hands: Its life expectancy is about 100 years. Here are some animals that usually live rather long lives.

ANIMAL	LIFE EXPECTANCY (IN YEARS)	ANIMAL	LIFE EXPECTANCY (IN YEARS)
Box turtle	100	Gorilla	20
Killer whale	90	Horse	20
Blue whale	80	Polar bear	20
Andean condor	70	White rhinoceros	20
Eclecus parrot	50	Black bear	18
Asian elephant	40	Black rhinoceros	15
Bald eagle	30	Lion	15
Hippopotamus	30	Lobster	15
Grizzly bear	25	Rhesus monkey	15

The box turtle is a kid compared to the quahog (*KOH-hog*), a type of clam that can live to be more than 200 years old.

Celebrity Animals

Rin Tin Tin, Trigger, Lassie, Flipper, Mickey Mouse, Snoopy . . . Animals real and imaginary have entertained us since the earliest days of movies and television. Here are some celebrity animals you might know.

Air Bud — Hoops-playing golden retriever from a movie

Babe — The pig from the movie of the same name

Beethoven — Saint Bernard dog from the movie of the same name

CatDog — Mixed-up cartoon animal

Clifford — Big red dog from books and TV

Dogbert — From the *Dilbert* comic strip

Garfield — The lasagna-loving cartoon cat

Keiko — The whale in *Free Willy*

Marcel — The monkey from *Friends*

Salem — The cat from *Sabrina the Teenage Witch*

Scooby-Doo — The cartoon dog

Shamu — The performing killer whale at Sea World

PsSST

A "talking" horse named **Mr. Ed** was one of the most famous celebrity animals. He starred in his own 1950s TV show. In the days before computer animation, stagehands used a small wire to make Mr. Ed "talk."

My Animals

Here's a place for you to list the animals in your life. You can list pets you have now, pets you once had, and there's a place for your favourite animals in the animal kingdom.

MY PETS

_____
_____
_____
_____
_____
_____
_____

MY FRIENDS' PETS

_____
_____
_____
_____
_____
_____

MY FAVOURITE ANIMALS

1. _____
2. _____
3. _____
4. _____
5. _____

CHAPTER TEN

Grab Bag

We took all the stuff that wouldn't fit anywhere else and shoved it into this chapter. So stick in your hand and see what you get! Good luck!

What's Your Sign?

Astrologists believe that the position of stars, moons, planets, and other heavenly bodies at the time of a person's birth influences his or her destiny. Here are the 12 signs of the zodiac. What's your sign?

SIGN	SYMBOL	DATES
Aquarius	Water carrier	Jan. 20 to Feb. 18
Pisces	Fish	Feb. 19 to Mar. 20
Aries	Ram	Mar. 21 to Apr. 20
Taurus	Bull	Apr. 21 to May 20
Gemini	Twins	May 21 to June 21
Cancer	Crab	June 22 to July 22
Leo	Lion	July 23 to Aug. 22
Virgo	Virgin	Aug. 23 to Sept. 22
Libra	Scales	Sept. 23 to Oct. 22
Scorpio	Scorpion	Oct. 23 to Nov. 21
Sagittarius	Archer	Nov. 22 to Dec. 20
Capricorn	Goat	Dec. 21 to Jan. 19

The earliest versions of astrology existed as long as 5,000 years ago. Early civilizations put great faith in the ability of the stars to predict the future.

What Animal Are You?

Just like the Western world's zodiac, the Chinese zodiac is divided into 12 signs. But each sign, which is the name of an animal, corresponds to one year, not just one month or so. Here are the animals of the Chinese zodiac and the years that they represent. What year were you born in?

ANIMAL SIGN	YEARS
Sheep	**1979, 1991, 2003, 2015**
Monkey	**1980, 1992, 2004, 2016**
Rooster	**1981, 1993, 2005, 2017**
Dog	**1982, 1994, 2006, 2018**
Boar	**1983, 1995, 2007, 2019**
Rat	**1972, 1984, 1996, 2008**
Ox	**1973, 1985, 1997, 2009**
Tiger	**1974, 1986, 1998, 2010**
Hare	**1975, 1987, 1999, 2011**
Dragon	**1976, 1988, 2000, 2012**
Snake	**1977, 1989, 2001, 2013**
Horse	**1978, 1990, 2002, 2014**

Some years are considered luckier than others. Occasionally, Chinese families try to make sure their babies are born during years of the dragon, for instance.

Nobel Peace Prize

The Peace Prize is one of six Nobel Prizes awarded annually (the others are for literature, physics, chemistry, medicine, and economics). The Peace Prize was first awarded in 1901. Here are the Peace winners since 1963. Note that the prize can go to a group or organization, not just one person.

1963 International Committee of the Red Cross; League of Red Cross Societies (Switzerland)

1964 Rev. Dr. Martin Luther King, Jr. (United States)

1965 UNICEF (United Nations Children's Fund)

1968 René Cassin (France)

1969 International Labour Organization

1970 Norman E. Borlaug (United States)

1971 Willy Brandt (West Germany)

1973 Henry A. Kissinger (United States); Le Duc Tho (North Vietnam; refused prize)

1974 Eisaku Sato (Japan); Sean MacBride (Ireland)

1975 Andrei D. Sakharov (U.S.S.R.)

1976 Mairead Corrigan and Betty Williams (Northern Ireland)

1977 Amnesty International

1978 Menachem Begin (Israel) and Anwar el-Sadat (Egypt)

1979 Mother Teresa of Calcutta (India)

1980 Adolfo Pérez Esquivel (Argentina)

1981 Office of the United Nations High Commissioner for Refugees

1982 Alva Myrdal (Sweden) and Alfonso García Robles (Mexico)

1983 Lech Walesa (Poland)

1984 Bishop Desmond Tutu (South Africa)

1985 International Physicians for the Prevention of Nuclear War

1986 Elie Wiesel (United States)

1987 Oscar Arias Sánchez (Costa Rica)

1988 U.N. Peacekeeping Forces

1989 Dalai Lama (Tibet)

1990 Mikhail S. Gorbachev (U.S.S.R.)

1991 Daw Aung San Suu Kyi (Burma)

1992 Rigoberta Menchú (Guatemala)

1993 F. W. de Klerk and Nelson Mandela (South Africa)

1994 Yasser Arafat (Palestine), and Shimon Peres and Yitzhak Rabin (Israel)

1995 Joseph Rotblat and Pugwash Conference on Science and World Affairs (U.K.)

1996 Carlos Filipe Ximenes Belo and José Ramos-Horta (both East Timor)

1997 Jody Williams and the International Campaign to Ban Landmines (United States)

1998 John Hume and David Trimble (both Northern Ireland)

1999 Doctors Without Borders (France)

2000 Kim Dae Jung (South Korea)

2001 United Nations and Secretary-General Kofi Annan

2002 Jimmy Carter, Jr. (United States)

2003 Shirin Ebadi (Iran)

2004 Wangari Maathai (Kenya)

What Canadian prime minister won the 1957 Nobel Peace Prize for his work in helping to set up a U.N. Peacekeeping Force?

Answer: Lester B. Pearson

Unusual Special Events

Canadians have lots of chances to get together throughout the year for some rather unusual special days and events. Here are just a few of the entertaining local celebrations held throughout the year, and the month in which they usually take place.

EVENT	LOCATION	MONTH
Ice Hotel Opening Day	Duchesnay, QC	January
Polar Bear Swims	Canada-wide	January
Cars on Ice Racing	Sherbrooke, QC	February
Red Nose Day	Canada-wide	February
High Five Day	Canada-wide	April
Black Fly Hunt	South River, ON	May-June
World's Longest Canoe Race	Yukon Territory	June
Giant Omelette Festival	Granby, QC	June
Bathtub Boat Races	Nanaimo, BC	July
Silly Summer Parade Day	Old Strathcona, AB	July
Just for Laughs Festival	Montreal, QC	July
International Outhouse Race	Dawson City, YT	August
Rock Paper Scissors Championship	Toronto, ON	October

A lot of equally entertaining special events also take place each year in the United States. Our favourites include Fruitcake Tossing (January, Colorado), Snow Shovel Racing (February, New Mexico), Stinky Rotten Sneakers Contest (March, Vermont), Cow Pasture Golf (September, Arizona), and Pumpkin Chucking (November, Delaware).

Dig These!

You're probably too young to remember most of the items on this list. But ask your mom, dad, grandma, or grandpa if they wore any of these out-of-date fad items — or if any of the clothes are hiding in their closets!

Acid-washed jeans

Bell-bottom pants

Go-go boots

Hot pants

Knickers

Leisure suits

Nehru jackets

Pedal pushers

Pillbox hats

Poodle skirts

Saddle shoes

Zoot suits

Nehru jackets, named for Indian prime minister Jawaharlal Nehru, had a banded collar and no lapels. They became a fashion hit after the Beatles took to wearing them in the 1960s.

Best-selling Cars

The Honda Civic was the best-selling passenger car in Canada in 2004, with more than 60,000 vehicles sold. But at that rate, it would take 366 years to equal the sales of the Toyota Corolla, the best-selling car in history. Here are the all-time most popular cars worldwide.

CAR	TOTAL SOLD	1ST YEAR AVAILABLE
Toyota Corolla	22 million	1963
Volkswagen Beetle	21 million	1937
Ford Model T	15.5 million	1908
Volkswagen Golf/Rabbit	15 million	1974
Lada Riva	13.5 million	1970

A Box of Lemons

According to the readers at CarTalk.com, here are the five worst cars of all time. Not the worst-selling — just the worst to own or drive, said the people who voted. Any of these in your garage?

1. Yugo
2. Chevy Vega
3. Ford Pinto
4. AMC Gremlin
5. Chevy Chevette

Volkswagen stopped production of the Beetle in the late 1970s, but the "Bug" made a comeback in 1998 and once again became a popular car.

Biggest Trucks

Is it just us, or do trucks rule? Seriously, doesn't every kid want a big, giant truck to drive to school? Okay, maybe not every kid, but we're guessing it's a lot. Anyway, here are some of the biggest trucks in the world.

Largest Dump Truck

T-282 (made by Liebherr Mining Equipment Co.)
It can carry more than 317,000 kg (700,000 lb.).

Largest Crane

Demag CC 12600 (made by Demag Mobile Cranes)
Height: 169 m (557 feet). It can lift 1.45 million kg (1,600 tons).

Largest Land Vehicle

RB293 Bucket-wheel Excavator (made by Man Takraf)
This earthmover is 220 m (722 feet) long, 94 m (310 feet) tall, and weighs 14 million kg (31 million lb.).

Largest Monster Truck

Bigfoot 5 (built by Bob Chandler)
More than 4.5 m (15 feet) tall; weighs 17,235 kg (38,000 lb.); has tires 3 m (10 feet) high.

The RB293 Bucket-wheel Excavator can shift nearly 240,000 cubic metres (8.5 million cubic feet) of earth per day. Think what that could do at your school yard!

That Is a *Big* Donut!

Wonder what the world's largest culinary creations are? Here's a tasting.

Largest Bowl of Soup/234.6 l (61.99 gallons)
It was beef and vegetable soup.

Largest Hamburger/7.31 m (24 feet) wide
It weighed 2,740 kg (6,040 lb.) and took two hours to cook.

Largest Chocolate Bar/2,358 kg (5,206 lb.)
It was the equivalent of 22,800 113-gram (four-ounce) bars.

Largest Cookie/26.6 m (81 feet, 9 inches) around
It was chocolate chip, of course.

Largest Donut/1,700 kg (3,739 lb.)
It was more than 4.6 m (15 feet) across!

Longest Hot Dog/4.1 m (13 feet, 4 inches)
It weighed more than 90 kg (200 lb.) and came complete with bun, mustard, ketchup, and pickles.

Largest Jar of Jelly Beans/2,744 kg (6,050 lb.)
It included 2,160,000 Jelly Belly candies.

Largest Pizza/37.3 m (122 feet, 8 inches) across
It contained nearly 1,818 kg (4,000 lb.) of cheese.

Largest Popsicle/9,080 kg (20,020 lb.)
It was 6.3 m (21 feet) long, 1.7 m (7 feet 5 inches) wide, and was an average of .86 m (3 feet 7 inches) thick.

Largest S'more/357 kg (789 lb.)
It included more than 9,000 toasted marshmallows.

Largest Sushi Roll/2,200 kg (4,851 lb.)
It stretched for 1.2 km (three quarters of a mile).

The world's largest food fight is an annual event in Buñol, Spain, called La Tomatina. In 1999, 25,000 people hurled more than a quarter million tomatoes in an hour!

Foods of the World

You'd be right at home eating the following foods in their native countries. Of course, if you've been to any of those big, fancy food courts at the mall, you could probably find a lot of these things right there.

Australia
Meat pie

China
Egg roll

England
Fish and chips

France
Brie

Germany
Bratwurst

Greece
Baklava

Hungary
Goulash

India
Curry

Ireland
Corned beef and cabbage

Israel
Matzo

Italy
Pizza

Jamaica
Jerk chicken

Japan
Sushi

Mexico
Burrito

Nigeria
Fufu

Philippines
Adobo

Poland
Kielbasa

Russia
Borscht

Spain
Paella

Sweden
Gravlax

Thailand
Pad thai noodles

Turkey
Shish kebab

USA
Barbecue

People in many countries enjoy pancakes, or something like them, for breakfast. They're sweeter thanks to Canada, which produces 80 percent of the world's maple syrup.

Gross Stuff People Eat

Warning: Don't try these at home . . . unless you're really brave! No, it isn't the menu for the next edition of *Survivor*. People enjoy these treats in countries all over the world. Listed with each food is just one of the countries where you can taste these delicacies.

FOOD/COUNTRY

Beef tongue and brains/Mexico

Chocolate-covered ants/United States

Cricket lollipops/United States

Deep-fried beetles/Thailand

Dog stew/South Korea

Dried sea slugs/China

Fried locusts/Thailand

Grasshopper paste/Zambia

Iguana soup/Mexico

Pigeon stew/Thailand

Sheep eyeballs/India

Tarantula kebabs/Cambodia

Toasted termites/South Africa

Edible snails are considered a delicacy even in Canada. Of course, they sound a lot more appetizing when they're smothered in garlic and butter — and called *escargot*!

Fruity Veggies

"But I ate all my vegetables!" you say. Well, maybe yes, maybe no. Maybe it wasn't really a vegetable. Here are some sneaky, common fruits often mistaken for vegetables. Don't let Mom see this list!

Avocado
Corn
Cucumbers
Eggplant
Green beans
Melons
Okra
Peppers
Pumpkins
Squash
Tomatoes

The technical definition of a fruit is "the ripened ovary of a seed-bearing plant." Corn, for instance, is actually a fruit because each kernel comes from the ovary of one corn flower on the plant.

What's on That Pizza?!

Ah, pizza! Easily the world's greatest food. Add pepperoni and you've got all the major food groups in each slice. But while you're probably used to seeing sausage or peppers or onions on pizza, here's a list of what people in other countries slap on top of their pizza pies.

COUNTRY	TOPPING
Australia	Eggs, shrimp
Bahamas	Barbecued chicken
Brazil	Green peas
Chile	Mussels and clams
Colombia	Guava
Costa Rica	Coconut
England	Tuna and corn
France	Fresh cream
Guatemala	Black bean sauce
India	Pickled ginger
Japan	Squid, mayonnaise, potato
Morocco	Lamb
Netherlands	Shwarma (grilled lamb)
Pakistan	Curry
Russia	Red herring

Hold the anchovies! The list of favourite pizza toppings varies from establishment to establishment, but almost every one ranks the small fish as the least popular topping.

World's Stinkiest Cheeses

Phew! Here's a list of the stinkiest cheeses in the world, according to people who love cheese, no matter how it smells! All these cheeses are from France, with the exception of Appenzeller, which is made in Switzerland, and Limburger, from Germany.

Appenzeller

Banon

Brie de Meaux

Camembert au Calvados

Epoisses

Limburger

Livarot

Muenster

Ossan Iraty

Pont l'Eveque

Raclette

Reblochon

Roquefort

Vieux Boulogne

According to *Wine X Magazine*, virtually all stinky cheeses are made from cow's milk, though goat and sheep cheeses also can be especially pungent.

Take a Day

You probably already know some of these holidays. But it can't hurt to learn a few more — think you can talk your teacher into giving you Guy Fawkes Day or Bastille Day off school?

DATE	HOLIDAY/COUNTRY
January 15	**Adults' Day**/Japan For people turning 20, making them adults
Jan./Feb.*	**Vietnamese New Year**/Vietnam A seven-day festival called *Tet Nguyen Dan*
February*	**Full Moon Day**/India and elsewhere Commemorates Buddhist teachings
February 6	**Waitangi Day**/New Zealand Recalls 1840 treaty signed by native Maori people
April*	**Sechseläuten**/Switzerland Celebrates the beginning of spring
May 5	**Children's Day**/Japan An official day to celebrate kids? Cool!
May 5	**Cinco de Mayo**/Mexico Celebrates 1861 victory over the French military
May 24*	**Victoria Day**/Canada Birthday of late Queen Victoria of Great Britain

Off, World!

DATE	HOLIDAY/COUNTRY
July 1	**King Kamehameha I Day**/Hawaii Honours first king to rule all of Hawaii's islands
July 1	**Canada Day**/Canada Honours creation of Canadian nation in 1867
July 14	**Bastille Day**/France Celebrates start of French Revolution in 1789
July/Aug.*	**Brother and Sister Day**/India Day that siblings have to be nice to one another
November 1-2	**Day of the Dead**/Mexico Honours ancestors and others who have died
November 5	**Guy Fawkes Day**/Great Britain Celebrates foiling of traitorous plot in 1605
December*	**Las Posadas**/Mexico Celebrates the coming of Christmas
December 26	**Boxing Day**/Gt. Britain, Canada, Australia A bonus day for giving gifts after Christmas

* These holidays are celebrated on different days each year, usually in the months listed.

In Japan, there used to be one holiday for girls and one for boys, but in 1948, they put them together. On Children's Day, kids go to shows, get new toys, and make cool crafts.

Easy Magic Tricks

Like almost anything else, it takes a lot of practice to become a skilled magician. But here are a few simple tricks you can start out with to amaze your friends and family.

MAGIC FINGERS

Ask someone to interlock his fingers and squeeze tightly. After a minute or so, have him or her stick his index fingers straight out while leaving his hands clasped together. The fingers should not be touching. Wave your hand over them and watch the fingers magically move toward each other. Try this one with your own hands first.

COLOUR YOUR MIND

You need six crayons of different colours. Put the crayons on a table. Gather your audience in front of you. Put your hands behind your back, then turn your back and ask someone to hand you one crayon and hide the rest. Tell your audience that you will now read their minds and reveal what crayon is in your hands. Here's the secret. With your thumb, scratch off a very tiny part of the crayon you're holding. While keeping the crayon in the *other* hand, turn around and put your hand on someone's head to "read" their mind." As you do it, carefully sneak a look at your thumb and see the colour you've scratched on your thumbnail. Build up the suspense by acting like you're "sensing" the colour, then reveal the answer.

SIMPLE CARD TRICK

Look at the deck and pick out your "favourite card." Set it aside face down on the table. Ask someone to pick a favourite card from the deck. Cut the deck and have the card placed on the top half. Put the bottom half over the top half. Cut the deck several times, then place your card anywhere in the middle. Cut it again. Tell him your favourite card. His will be right next to it in the deck. How does it work? Because the card you choose as your favourite isn't really the one you took out of the deck. It's actually the top card of the deck, which you need to note mentally and tell him that it was your "favourite."

The secret to most magic tricks is that the audience members don't see everything that happens — and they believe they see things that don't really happen.

Famous Magicians

Harry Houdini, an escape artist in the 1920s, is perhaps the best-known magician in history. Here are some other famous magicians who have baffled audiences with feats of illusion, along with some of their specialties.

John Henry Anderson   first to pull rabbit from a hat

Harry Blackstone, Sr.   expert in large illusions

Joseph Buatier famous for disappearing birdcage trick

David Copperfield   makes big things disappear

Adelaide Hermann   late 19th century female magician

Alexander Hermann   famous for "dancing pants" illusion

Doug Henning   popular on TV in the 1970s

Harry Houdini   world's greatest escape artist

Servais LeRoy   Belgian inventor of magic tricks

John Maskelyne   created levitation (floating body) trick

Penn and Teller   combine comedy and magic

Giuseppe Pinetti   used robotlike machines in tricks

Jean Robert-Houdin   created stage magic, invented tricks

Siegfried & Roy   used white tigers in their shows

Chung Ling Soo   died trying to catch bullet in his teeth

Howard Thurston   made cars vanish, people float

PsSST

Chung Ling Soo was a world-renowned magician in the early 1900s. Perhaps his greatest illusion was the fact that he really was an American named William Robinson!

Packing for Camping

We know you'll remember to bring a tent and a sleeping bag the next time you're ready for the great outdoors. But a good camping list also includes — but is not limited to — these items.

Batteries

Camera and film

Cooking/eating utensils

First-aid kit

Fishing gear

Food

Games/Cards

Hiking boots

Insect repellent

Lantern (or flashlight)

Matches (or a lighter)

Plastic garbage bags

Plastic tarp

Radio

Rain gear

Rope

Sewing kit

Soap, toilet paper, deodorant

Sunglasses

Sunscreen

Swiss Army knife

Toothpaste and toothbrush

Water

Don't forget the ingredients you'll need to make S'mores, everyone's favourite camping dessert: graham crackers, chocolate bars, and marshmallows. Roast the biggest marshmallow you can find and stick it on top of a chocolate bar between two graham crackers. It's gooey, but it's good — and you'll definitely want "some more"!

Space Junk

Space agencies provide just about everything an astronaut needs on his or her flight into space. But astronauts also can carry some personal items aboard. Here are a few unusual items that have travelled in space, according to *Air & Space/Smithsonian Magazine* and other sources.

Astrolabe (a navigation tool) from the 17th century

Bible on microfilm

Corned-beef **sandwich**

Doorknob from the Wisconsin state capitol

Four-star **insignia** of U.S. General Omar Bradley

Hand fan used by officials in sumo wrestling matches

Silk socks worn by Cornell University President Ezra Cornell in 1831

Small **piece of Stonehenge**, the ancient stone monument in Great Britain

Spurs owned by President Ronald Reagan

A **sternpost** from Captain James Cook's ship *Endeavour*

Swatch of **fabric** from the Wright brothers' first airplane

Vial of **sand** from Kitty Hawk, North Carolina, site of the Wright brothers' first flight

Astronaut Alan Shepard carried golf balls along on the *Apollo 14* mission. He needed something to hit them with, so he attached the head of a 6-iron to a tool handle and swung away on the moon!

My Food

This chapter had several food-related lists. Here's another one. In the spaces below, fill out these food categories. If you get too hungry while you're doing it, please — stop and get a snack. We don't want anybody fainting . . .

My number-one favourite food _____

My least favourite food _____

My favourite snack _____

My favourite drink _____

My favourite vegetable* _____

My favourite sandwich _____

My favourite thing my mom makes _____

My favourite school lunch _____

I've eaten more of this than anything else _____

I wouldn't eat this if you paid me a million dollars _____

Someday, I'd like to try this _____

BONUS:

My pet's favourite treat _____

My parents' favourite snack _____

Grossest thing I've ever eaten* _____

* C'mon — surely there's at least one!

Do you know how many calories a person is supposed to consume every day to make a healthy diet? About 500, 2,000, or 5,000?

Answer: 2,000 calories is a good number to shoot for. And not all from candy!

CHAPTER ELEVEN

Sports

Kick it, throw it, pass it, catch it, ride it, drive it, surf it . . . whatever you like to do in the world of sports, you'll find it in here. We've got the winners of all the big events, the champions from all the big sports, and even the story of what Inuits do with their ears. Really!

NBA Champions

The NBA was formed officially in 1948 with the merger of the National Basketball League and the American Basketball Association. The Boston Celtics have won the most titles with 16.

1946–47 Philadelphia Warriors	**1976–77** Portland Trail Blazers
1947–48 Philadelphia Warriors	**1977–78** Washington Bullets
1948–49 Minneapolis Lakers	**1978–79** Seattle SuperSonics
1949–50 Minneapolis Lakers	**1979–80** Los Angeles Lakers
1950–51 Rochester Royals	**1980–81** Boston Celtics
1951–52 Minneapolis Lakers	**1981–82** Los Angeles Lakers
1952–53 Minneapolis Lakers	**1982–83** Philadelphia 76ers
1953–54 Minneapolis Lakers	**1983–84** Boston Celtics
1954–55 Syracuse Nationals	**1984–85** Los Angeles Lakers
1955–56 Philadelphia Warriors	**1985–86** Boston Celtics
1956–57 Boston Celtics	**1986–87** Los Angeles Lakers
1957–58 St. Louis Hawks	**1987–88** Los Angeles Lakers
1958–59 Boston Celtics	**1988–89** Detroit Pistons
1959–60 Boston Celtics	**1989–90** Detroit Pistons
1960–61 Boston Celtics	**1990–91** Chicago Bulls
1961–62 Boston Celtics	**1991–92** Chicago Bulls
1962–63 Boston Celtics	**1992–93** Chicago Bulls
1963–64 Boston Celtics	**1993–94** Houston Rockets
1964–65 Boston Celtics	**1994–95** Houston Rockets
1965–66 Boston Celtics	**1995–96** Chicago Bulls
1966–67 Philadelphia 76ers	**1996–97** Chicago Bulls
1967–68 Boston Celtics	**1997–98** Chicago Bulls
1968–69 Boston Celtics	**1998–99** San Antonio Spurs
1969–70 New York Knicks	**1999–2000** Los Angeles Lakers
1970–71 Milwaukee Bucks	**2000–01** Los Angeles Lakers
1971–72 Los Angeles Lakers	**2001–02** Los Angeles Lakers
1972–73 New York Knicks	**2002–03** San Antonio Spurs
1973–74 Boston Celtics	**2003–04** Detroit Pistons
1974–75 Golden State Warriors	**2004–05** San Antonio Spurs
1975–76 Boston Celtics	**2005–06**

Now you'll know why the Lakers are called the Lakers when there aren't really any lakes in Los Angeles: Minnesota, the team's original home, is called the "Land of 10,000 Lakes."

Scoring Machines

Rack 'em up. Fill the bucket. From downtown. With authority. However you say it, scoring is the name of the game in basketball. Here are the all-time highest scorers in the NBA.

PLAYER	POINTS
Kareem Abdul-Jabbar	38,387
Karl Malone	36,928
Michael Jordan	32,292
Wilt Chamberlain	31,149
Moses Malone	27,409
Elvin Hayes	27,313
Hakeem Olajuwon	26,946
Oscar Robertson	26,710
Dominique Wilkins	26,688
John Havlicek	26,395
Alex English	25,613
Jerry West	25,192
Reggie Miller*	24,907
Patrick Ewing	24,708
Charles Barkley	23,757

(*Still active through 2004–2005 season.)

It's no surprise that Wilt "the Stilt" Chamberlain is among the all-time scoring leaders. He once averaged 50.4 points per game for an entire season! He scored 40 or more points in a game 271 times. And he is the only NBA player to score 100 points in a single game, which he did in 1962.

A National Pastime

While ice hockey might be Canada's favourite spectator sport, another icy activity—curling—attracts millions of fans and players, too. While most players take part for fun, some excel and take part in competitions. Here are some facts from Canada's curling national championships.

THE BRIER CUP

First awarded in 1927, the Brier is the top trophy awarded to Canadian men's teams. Here's a list of how many Briers each region has won:

PROVINCE	BRIER CUPS	MOST RECENT
Manitoba	26	1999
Alberta	21	2003
Ontario	8	1998
Saskatchewan	7	1980
Northern Ontario	4	1985
British Columbia	4	2000
Nova Scotia	3	2004
Newfoundland	1	1976
Quebec	1	1977

WOMEN'S CHAMPIONSHIP

The women's teams have competed in a national championship since 1961. Here are the most successful provinces:

PROVINCE	TITLES	MOST RECENT
Saskatchewan	10	1997
British Columbia	8	2000
Manitoba	6	1995
Alberta	5	1998

While Manitoba and Alberta have dominated the men's competition, the all-time leader for most appearances by a player is Russ Hodges, who was the skip of the Ontario or New Brunswick teams 13 times through 2004.

Tennis Grand Slams

The four "major" tennis tournaments are the Australian, French, and U.S. Opens, and Wimbledon, played in England. Both male and female tennis players are compared through the years on how many of these "Grand Slam" tournaments they win. Here are the top Grand Slam singles-title winners for both men and women.

WOMEN

PLAYER	AUSTRALIAN	FRENCH	U.S.	WIMBLEDON	TOTAL
Margaret Smith Court	11	5	5	3	24
Steffi Graf	4	6	5	7	22
Helen Wills Moody	0	4	7	8	19
Chris Evert	2	7	6	3	18
Martina Navratilova	3	2	9	4	18

MEN

PLAYER	AUSTRALIAN	FRENCH	U.S.	WIMBLEDON	TOTAL
Pete Sampras	2	0	5	7	14
Roy Emerson	6	2	2	2	12
Bjorn Borg	0	6	0	5	11
Rod Laver	3	2	2	4	11
Bill Tilden	0	0	7	3	10

Perhaps the greatest feat in tennis is winning all four Grand Slam events in one calendar year. Rod Laver accomplished it in 1962 and 1968. For the women, Margaret Smith Court did it in 1970, and Steffi Graf aced a clean sweep in 1988.

World Series Winners

The champions of Major League Baseball are the winners of the annual World Series, played between the winners of the National and American leagues. The New York Yankees have won the most World Series with 26, almost three times as many as the next-best total.

1903	Boston Pilgrims	1928	New York Yankees
1904	No series	1929	Philadelphia Athletics
1905	New York Giants	1930	Philadelphia Athletics
1906	Chicago White Sox	1931	St. Louis Cardinals
1907	Chicago Cubs	1932	New York Yankees
1908	Chicago Cubs	1933	New York Giants
1909	Pittsburgh Pirates	1934	St. Louis Cardinals
1910	Philadelphia Athletics	1935	Detroit Tigers
1911	Philadelphia Athletics	1936	New York Yankees
1912	Boston Red Sox	1937	New York Yankees
1913	Philadelphia Athletics	1938	New York Yankees
1914	Boston Braves	1939	New York Yankees
1915	Boston Red Sox	1940	Cincinnati Reds
1916	Boston Red Sox	1941	New York Yankees
1917	Chicago White Sox	1942	St. Louis Cardinals
1918	Boston Red Sox	1943	New York Yankees
1919	Cincinnati Reds	1944	St. Louis Cardinals
1920	Cleveland Indians	1945	Detroit Tigers
1921	New York Giants	1946	St. Louis Cardinals
1922	New York Giants	1947	New York Yankees
1923	New York Yankees	1948	Cleveland Indians
1924	Washington Senators	1949	New York Yankees
1925	Pittsburgh Pirates	1950	New York Yankees
1926	St. Louis Cardinals	1951	New York Yankees
1927	New York Yankees	1952	New York Yankees

1953	New York Yankees	1980	Philadelphia Phillies
1954	New York Giants	1981	Los Angeles Dodgers
1955	Brooklyn Dodgers	1982	St. Louis Cardinals
1956	New York Yankees	1983	Baltimore Orioles
1957	Milwaukee Braves	1984	Detroit Tigers
1958	New York Yankees	1985	Kansas City Royals
1959	Los Angeles Dodgers	1986	New York Mets
1960	Pittsburgh Pirates	1987	Minnesota Twins
1961	New York Yankees	1988	Los Angeles Dodgers
1962	New York Yankees	1989	Oakland Athletics
1963	Los Angeles Dodgers	1990	Cincinnati Reds
1964	St. Louis Cardinals	1991	Minnesota Twins
1965	Los Angeles Dodgers	1992	Toronto Blue Jays
1966	Baltimore Orioles	1993	Toronto Blue Jays
1967	St. Louis Cardinals	1994	No series
1968	Detroit Tigers	1995	Atlanta Braves
1969	New York Mets	1996	New York Yankees
1970	Baltimore Orioles	1997	Florida Marlins
1971	Pittsburgh Pirates	1998	New York Yankees
1972	Oakland Athletics	1999	New York Yankees
1973	Oakland Athletics	2000	New York Yankees
1974	Oakland Athletics	2001	Arizona Diamondbacks
1975	Cincinnati Reds	2002	Anaheim Angels
1976	Cincinnati Reds	2003	Florida Marlins
1977	New York Yankees	2004	Boston Red Sox
1978	New York Yankees	2005	
1979	Pittsburgh Pirates	2006	

The World Series was not held in 1904 because of a dispute between the leagues. It was cancelled in 1994 because of a labour strike by players.

Super Bowls

The National Football League began in 1920. Through 1932, the champion simply had the best regular-season record. From 1933 to 1965, the NFL Championship Game determined who was number one. Since then, the new Super Bowl has been played to decide what team was the NFL champion. Here is the list of all the Super Bowl champs with the season for which they were champions.

1966	Green Bay Packers	1987	Washington Redskins
1967	Green Bay Packers	1988	San Francisco 49ers
1968	New York Jets	1989	San Francisco 49ers
1969	Kansas City Chiefs	1990	New York Giants
1970	Baltimore Colts	1991	Washington Redskins
1971	Dallas Cowboys	1992	Dallas Cowboys
1972	Miami Dolphins	1993	Dallas Cowboys
1973	Miami Dolphins	1994	San Francisco 49ers
1974	Pittsburgh Steelers	1995	Dallas Cowboys
1975	Pittsburgh Steelers	1996	Green Bay Packers
1976	Oakland Raiders	1997	Denver Broncos
1977	Dallas Cowboys	1998	Denver Broncos
1978	Pittsburgh Steelers	1999	St. Louis Rams
1979	Pittsburgh Steelers	2000	Baltimore Ravens
1980	Oakland Raiders	2001	New England Patriots
1981	San Francisco 49ers	2002	Tampa Bay Buccaneers
1982	Washington Redskins	2003	New England Patriots
1983	Los Angeles Raiders	2004	New England Patriots
1984	San Francisco 49ers	2005	
1985	Chicago Bears	2006	
1986	New York Giants	2007	

What secret weapon did the New York Giants use to win the 1934 NFL Championship Game?

They switched from football cleats to sneakers in the second half, and had better traction on the frozen field than the Chicago Bears. Good call!

Canadian Football League

Canadian football, as played in the CFL, developed about the same time as the American version, but with slightly different rules and field dimensions. Listed below are the nine current teams in the CFL, along with the year the team or its rugby-club ancestors first played.

TEAM	YEAR FOUNDED
British Columbia Lions	1951
Edmonton Eskimos	1892
Calgary Stampeders	1935
Hamilton Tiger-Cats	1869
Montréal Alouettes	1946
Ottawa Renegades	2002
Saskatchewan Roughriders	1910
Toronto Argonauts	1873
Winnipeg Blue Bombers	1879

Grey Cup Titles

The Grey Cup was first awarded in 1909. Since 1954, it has gone to the Canadian Football League champion. Here are the CFL teams that have won the most Grey Cups since 1954:

Edmonton	12	Hamilton	7	Winnipeg	7
Ottawa (Rough Riders)	5	Toronto	5		

The CFL tried an experiment in the 1990s by adding seven teams that played in the United States. They were in cities in Texas, Lousiana, Nevada, and other states. Can you name the only American team to win the Grey Cup, which it did in 1995?

Answer: Baltimore Stallions

World Cup Winners

The biggest sporting event in the world is not the Olympics. It's the World Cup of soccer, held every four years in a different country. More than 180 nations compete in the two-year tournament that sends 32 teams to the final playoffs. The World Cup final is always the most-watched sporting event of the year worldwide.

YEAR	CHAMPION	HOST COUNTRIES
1930	Uruguay	Uruguay
1934	Italy	Italy
1938	Italy	France
1950	Uruguay	Brazil
1954	W. Germany	Switzerland
1958	Brazil	Sweden
1962	Brazil	Chile
1966	England	England
1970	Brazil	Mexico
1974	Germany	Germany
1978	Argentina	Argentina
1982	Italy	Spain
1986	Argentina	Mexico
1990	Germany	Italy
1994	Brazil	United States
1998	France	France
2002	Brazil	Korea and Japan

Canada's national women's soccer team has taken part in three Women's World Cups, which started in 1991. In 2003, they finished in fourth place, their best result ever.

Canadians Go Global

Canadian pro soccer players looking to improve their games and play in the world's best leagues head overseas, in most cases, to further their careers. Through the middle of 2005, here is a list of some prominent Canadian players making their marks in some of the toughest national leagues of other countries. Look for many of these players to try to help Canada earn a berth in the 2006 World Cup.

PLAYER	POSITION	COUNTRY
Fernando Aguiar	Midfield	Portugal
Marc Bircham	Midfield	England
Jim Brennan	Midfield	England
Dwayne deRosario	Forward	U.S.
Jason DeVos	Defense	England
Lars Hirschfeld	Goal	England
Iain Hume	Forward	England
Atiba Hutchinson	Midfield	Sweden
Daniel Imhof	Midfield	Switzerland
Kevin McKenna	Defense	Scotland
Tony Menezes	Defense	China
Tomasz Radzinski	Forward	England
Paul Stalteri	Defense	Germany

The high point in Canadian soccer history probably came in 1985, when the team defeated Honduras 2-1. The victory earned Canada its first berth in the World Cup, held in 1986 in Mexico. Another huge win came in the 2000 Gold Cup, where Canada defeated Mexico and Colombia to capture the tournament title.

Hockey's Best

The champions of the National Hockey League receive the Stanley Cup, the oldest trophy in professional sports. The cup was created in 1893 for Canada's amateur hockey leagues. In 1917 the NHL was officially formed and its teams began to compete for it. By 1926, only NHL teams could compete for the cup.

1917	Seattle Metropolitans	1941	Boston Bruins
1918	Toronto Arenas	1942	Toronto Maple Leafs
1919	Montreal-Seattle*	1943	Detroit Red Wings
1920	Ottawa Senators	1944	Montreal Canadiens
1921	Ottawa Senators	1945	Toronto Maple Leafs
1922	Toronto St. Pats	1946	Montreal Canadiens
1923	Ottawa Senators	1947	Toronto Maple Leafs
1924	Montreal Maroons	1948	Toronto Maple Leafs
1925	Victoria Athletic Club	1949	Toronto Maple Leafs
1926	Montreal Maroons	1950	Detroit Red Wings
1927	Ottawa Senators	1951	Toronto Maple Leafs
1928	New York Rangers	1952	Detroit Red Wings
1929	Boston Bruins	1953	Montreal Canadiens
1930	Montreal Canadiens	1954	Detroit Red Wings
1931	Montreal Canadiens	1955	Detroit Red Wings
1932	Toronto Maple Leafs	1956	Montreal Canadiens
1933	New York Rangers	1957	Montreal Canadiens
1934	Chicago Blackhawks	1958	Montreal Canadiens
1935	Montreal Maroons	1959	Montreal Canadiens
1936	Detroit Red Wings	1960	Montreal Canadiens
1937	Detroit Red Wings	1961	Chicago Blackhawks
1938	Chicago Blackhawks	1962	Toronto Maple Leafs
1939	Boston Bruins	1963	Toronto Maple Leafs
1940	New York Rangers	1964	Toronto Maple Leafs

 Each member of a Stanley Cup-winning team gets to take the cup itself home for one day after the NHL Finals. Some players drink out of the cup, give babies baths in it, or take it to cheer up sick kids in hospitals.

1965	Montreal Canadiens	1987	Edmonton Oilers
1966	Montreal Canadiens	1988	Edmonton Oilers
1967	Toronto Maple Leafs	1989	Calgary Flames
1968	Montreal Canadiens	1990	Edmonton Oilers
1969	Montreal Canadiens	1991	Pittsburgh Penguins
1970	Boston Bruins	1992	Pittsburgh Penguins
1971	Montreal Canadiens	1993	Montreal Canadiens
1972	Boston Bruins	1994	New York Rangers
1973	Montreal Canadiens	1995	New Jersey Devils
1974	Philadelphia Flyers	1996	Colorado Avalanche
1975	Philadelphia Flyers	1997	Detroit Red Wings
1976	Montreal Canadiens	1998	Detroit Red Wings
1977	Montreal Canadiens	1999	Dallas Stars
1978	Montreal Canadiens	2000	New Jersey Devils
1979	Montreal Canadiens	2001	Colorado Avalanche
1980	New York Islanders	2002	Detroit Red Wings
1981	New York Islanders	2003	New Jersey Devils
1982	New York Islanders	2004	Tampa Bay Lightning
1983	New York Islanders	2005	Season cancelled
1984	Edmonton Oilers	2006	
1985	Edmonton Oilers		
1986	Montreal Canadiens		

* The Cup was shared after a flu epidemic led to cancellation of the final playoff series.

He Shoots...He Scores!

In the National Hockey League, players who score a lot of goals are called "lamplighters." That's because a red light goes on behind the goal after a score. Here are the top ten goal-scorers in NHL history.

Wayne Gretzky	894	Mike Gartner	708
Gordie Howe	801	Mark Messier	694
Brett Hull*	741	Mario Lemieux*	683
Marcel Dionne	731	Steve Yzerman*	678
Phil Esposito	717	Luc Robitaille *	653

(* Still active. Stats through 2003–2004 season.)

MVP! MVP!

Since the end of the 1923–24 season, the National Hockey League has awarded the Hart Trophy to its most valuable player. The winner is selected by the Professional Hockey Writers' Association.

YEAR	PLAYER	TEAM
2003-04	Martin St. Louis	Tampa Bay Lightning
2002-03	Peter Forsberg	Colorado Avalanche
2001-02	José Théodore	Montreal Canadiens
2000-01	Joe Sakic	Colorado Avalanche
1999-2000	Chris Pronger	St. Louis Blues
1998-99	Jaromir Jagr	Pittsburgh Penguins
1997-98	Dominik Hasek	Buffalo Sabres
1996-97	Dominik Hasek	Buffalo Sabres
1995-96	Mario Lemieux	Pittsburgh Penguins
1994-95	Eric Lindros	Philadelphia Flyers
1993-94	Sergei Federov	Detroit Red Wings
1992-93	Mario Lemieux	Pittsburgh Penguins
1991-92	Mark Messier	New York Rangers
1990-91	Brett Hull	St. Louis Blues
1989-90	Mark Messier	Edmonton Oilers
1988-89	Wayne Gretzky	Los Angeles Kings
1987-88	Mario Lemieux	Pittsburgh Penguins
1986-87	Wayne Gretzky	Edmonton Oilers
1985-86	Wayne Gretzky	Edmonton Oilers
1984-85	Wayne Gretzky	Edmonton Oilers
1983-84	Wayne Gretzky	Edmonton Oilers
1982-83	Wayne Gretzky	Edmonton Oilers
1981-82	Wayne Gretzky	Edmonton Oilers
1980-81	Wayne Gretzky	Edmonton Oilers
1979-80	Wayne Gretzky	Edmonton Oilers
1978-79	Bryan Trottier	New York Islanders
1977-78	Guy Lafleur	Montreal Canadiens
1976-77	Guy Lafleur	Montreal Canadiens
1975-76	Bobby Clarke	Philadelphia Flyers
1974-75	Bobby Clarke	Philadelphia Flyers
1973-74	Phil Esposito	Boston Bruins
1972-73	Bobby Clarke	Philadelphia Flyers
1971-72	Bobby Orr	Boston Bruins
1970-71	Bobby Orr	Boston Bruins
1969-70	Bobby Orr	Boston Bruins
1968-69	Phil Esposito	Boston Bruins
1967-68	Stan Mikita	Chicago Blackhawks
1966-67	Stan Mikita	Chicago Blackhawks
1965-66	Bobby Hull	Chicago Blackhawks

YEAR	PLAYER	TEAM
1964-65	Bobby Hull	Chicago Blackhawks
1963-64	Jean Beliveau	Montreal Canadiens
1962-63	Gordie Howe	Detroit Red Wings
1961-62	Jacques Plante	Montreal Canadiens
1960-61	Bernie Geoffrion	Montreal Canadiens
1959-60	Gordie Howe	Detroit Red Wings
1958-59	Andy Bathgate	New York Rangers
1957-58	Gordie Howe	Detroit Red Wings
1956-57	Gordie Howe	Detroit Red Wings
1955-56	Jean Beliveau	Montreal Canadiens
1954-55	Ted Kennedy	Toronto Maple Leafs
1953-54	Al Rollins	Chicago Blackhawks
1952-53	Gordie Howe	Detroit Red Wings
1951-52	Gordie Howe	Detroit Red Wings
1950-51	Milt Schmidt	Boston Bruins
1949-50	Chuck Rayner	New York Rangers
1948-49	Sid Abel	Detroit Red Wings
1947-48	Buddy O'Connor	New York Rangers
1946-47	Maurice Richard	Montreal Canadiens
1945-46	Max Bentley	Chicago Blackhawks
1944-45	Elmer Lach	Montreal Canadiens
1943-44	Babe Pratt	Toronto Maple Leafs
1942-43	Bill Cowley	Boston Bruins
1941-42	Tom Anderson	New York Americans
1940-41	Bill Cowley	Boston Bruins
1939-40	Ebbie Goodfellow	Detroit Red Wings
1938-39	Toe Blake	Montreal Canadiens
1937-38	Eddie Shore	Boston Bruins
1936-37	Babe Siebert	Montreal Canadiens
1935-36	Eddie Shore	Boston Bruins
1934-35	Eddie Shore	Boston Bruins
1933-34	Aurel Joliat	Montreal Canadiens
1932-33	Eddie Shore	Boston Bruins
1931-32	Howie Morenz	Montreal Canadiens
1930-31	Howie Morenz	Montreal Canadiens
1929-30	Nels Stewart	Montreal Maroons
1928-29	Roy Worters	New York Americans
1927-28	Howie Morenz	Montreal Canadiens
1926-27	Herb Gardiner	Montreal Canadiens
1925-26	Nels Stewart	Montreal Maroons
1924-25	Billy Burch	Hamilton Tigers
1923-24	Frank Nighbor	Ottawa Senators

Who is the Hart Trophy named for?

Answer: Dr. David Hart, the father of former Montreal Canadiens coach and player Cecil Hart. Dr. Hart donated the trophy in 1923.

NASCAR Champions

Stock-car racing has become one of North America's fastest-growing sports. But those high-speed heroes have been racing around for more than 50 years. Here are the champions of NASCAR from the beginning. The top level of NASCAR racing is currently called the Nextel Cup Series.

YEAR	CAR NO.	DRIVER	YEAR	CAR NO.	DRIVER
1949	22	Red Byron	1977	11	Cale Yarborough
1950	60	Bill Rexford	1978	11	Cale Yarborough
1951	92	Herb Thomas	1979	43	Richard Petty
1952	91	Tim Flock	1980	2	Dale Earnhardt
1953	92	Herb Thomas	1981	11	Darrell Waltrip
1954	42	Lee Petty	1982	11	Darrell Waltrip
1955	300	Tim Flock	1983	22	Bobby Allison
1956	300	Buck Baker	1984	44	Terry Labonte
1957	87	Buck Baker	1985	11	Darrell Waltrip
1958	42	Lee Petty	1986	3	Dale Earnhardt
1959	42	Lee Petty	1987	3	Dale Earnhardt
1960	4	Rex White	1988	9	Bill Elliott
1961	11	Ned Jarrett	1989	27	Rusty Wallace
1962	8	Joe Weatherly	1990	3	Dale Earnhardt
1963	8	Joe Weatherly	1991	3	Dale Earnhardt
1964	43	Richard Petty	1992	7	Alan Kulwicki
1965	11	Ned Jarrett	1993	3	Dale Earnhardt
1966	6	David Pearson	1994	3	Dale Earnhardt
1967	43	Richard Petty	1995	24	Jeff Gordon
1968	17	David Pearson	1996	5	Terry Labonte
1969	17	David Pearson	1997	24	Jeff Gordon
1970	71	Bobby Isaac	1998	24	Jeff Gordon
1971	43	Richard Petty	1999	88	Dale Jarrett
1972	43	Richard Petty	2000	18	Bobby Labonte
1973	72	Benny Parsons	2001	24	Jeff Gordon
1974	43	Richard Petty	2002	20	Tony Stewart
1975	43	Richard Petty	2003	17	Matt Kenseth
1976	11	Cale Yarborough	2004	97	Kurt Busch

Nextel Cup drivers get points for everything from victories to laps led. In 2004, Kurt Busch won the title over Jimmie Johnson by just eight points, the tightest race ever.

Golf's Grand Slam

Four annual golf tournaments make up the famous "Grand Slam." No golfer has won the U.S. Open, British Open, Masters, and PGA Championship in one year, but Tiger Woods won all four in a row, over two years. The golfers listed here are the only ones to win all four tournaments during their career. Also listed are the golfers who have won each Grand Slam event the most times.

CAREER GRAND SLAM
(Number of wins per tournament)

GOLFER	MASTERS	U.S. OPEN	BRITISH OPEN	PGA
Jack Nicklaus	6	4	3	5
Ben Hogan	2	4	1	2
Gary Player	3	1	3	2
Tiger Woods	4	2	1	2
Gene Sarazen	1	2	1	3

MOST VICTORIES IN "MAJORS"

The Masters

Jack Nicklaus, 6
Arnold Palmer, 4
Tiger Woods, 4

U.S. Open

Jack Nicklaus, 4
Ben Hogan, 4
Bobby Jones, 4
Willie Anderson, 4

British Open

Harry Vardon, 6
Tom Watson, 5
J.H. Taylor, 5

PGA Championship

Walter Hagen, 5
Jack Nicklaus, 5
Gene Sarazen, 3
Sam Snead, 3

Unlike today's all-professional Grand Slam, the original included the U.S. and British Amateurs, along with the U.S. and British Opens. The great Bobby Jones was the only golfer to win an original Grand Slam (1927).

Triple Crown Horses

Thoroughbred horses that win the Kentucky Derby, Preakness, and Belmont Stakes races (all held in the United States) in one year earn the fabled Triple Crown. Only 11 horses have captured that prize. Only one jockey, Eddie Arcaro, has ridden two different horses to Triple Crowns.

YEAR	HORSE	JOCKEY
1919	Sir Barton	Johnny Loftus
1930	Gallant Fox	Earl Sande
1935	Omaha	Willie Saunders
1937	War Admiral	Charley Kurtsinger
1941	Whirlaway	Eddie Arcaro
1943	Count Fleet	Johnny Longden
1946	Assault	Warren Mehrtens
1948	Citation	Eddie Arcaro
1973	Secretariat	Ron Turcotte
1977	Seattle Slew	Jean Cruguet
1978	Affirmed	Steve Cauthen

In 1973, the mighty Secretariat won the Belmont Stakes by an incredible 31 "lengths." The distance between horses in a race is measured in lengths; that is, the distance from a horse's nose to its rear.

World's Fastest

The people who hold the record for the 100-metre (110-yard) dash are considered the "fastest man" and "fastest woman" in the world. The identities of those people change, of course, as people run faster and faster times. Here are the five most recent world-record times for men and women in track and field's fastest race.

ATHLETE, COUNTRY	YEAR	TIME*
MEN		
Asafa Powell, Jamaica	2005	9.77
Tim Montgomery, U.S.	2002	9.78
Maurice Greene, U.S.	1999	9.79
Donovan Bailey, Canada	1996**	9.84
Leroy Burrell, U.S.	1994	9.84
WOMEN		
Florence Griffith-Joyner, U.S.	1988	10.49
Evelyn Ashford, U.S.	1984	10.76
Evelyn Ashford, U.S.	1983	10.79
Marlies Göhr, East Germany	1983	10.81
Marlies Oelsner, East Germany	1977	10.88

* In seconds.   ** Record set while winning an Olympic gold medal.

Scientists have debated just how low these 100-metre times will go. Some feel that human beings are already reaching their full potential; that is, that we can't go much faster. However, scientists also said that about 50 years ago, when the women's record was 11.5 seconds!

Olympic History

The Olympics were first held more than 2,000 years ago in ancient Greece. A movement to restart the Games led to the first modern Olympics in 1896. Today, Olympics are held every two years, alternating Winter and Summer Games.

SUMMER GAMES

1896 Athens, Greece

1900 Paris, France

1904 St. Louis, U.S.

1906 Athens, Greece

1908 London, England

1912 Stockholm, Sweden

1920 Antwerp, Belgium

1924 Paris, France

1928 Amsterdam, Netherlands

1932 Los Angeles, U.S.

1936 Berlin, Germany

1948 London, England

1952 Helsinki, Finland

1956 Melbourne, Australia

1960 Rome, Italy

1964 Tokyo, Japan

1968 Mexico City, Mexico

1972 Munich, West Germany

Olympic Tug-of-War?

Over the years, some sports have been removed from the Olympics. Here are some sports that are no longer golden.

Cricket

Croquet

Jeu de paume (like tennis)

One-handed weightlifting

Polo

Rope climb

Standing long jump

Standing high jump

Tug-of-war

Underwater swimming

1976	Montreal, Canada	1996	Atlanta, U.S.
1980	Moscow, Soviet Union	2000	Sydney, Australia
1984	Los Angeles, U.S.	2004	Athens, Greece
1988	Seoul, South Korea	2008	Beijing, China*
1992	Barcelona, Spain	2012	London, England*

WINTER GAMES

1924	Chamonix, France	1972	Sapporo, Japan
1928	St. Moritz, Switzerland	1976	Innsbruck, Austria
1932	Lake Placid, U.S.	1980	Lake Placid, U.S.
1936	Garmisch-Partinkirchen, Germany	1984	Sarajevo, Yugoslavia
		1988	Calgary, Canada
1948	St. Moritz, Switzerland	1992	Albertville, France
1952	Oslo, Norway	1994	Lillehammer, Norway
1956	Cortina d'Ampezzo, Italy	1998	Nagano, Japan
1960	Squaw Valley, U.S.	2002	Salt Lake City, U.S.
1964	Innsbruck, Austria	2006	Turin, Italy*
1968	Grenoble, France	2010	Vancouver, Canada*

* Scheduled as of 2005

The Olympics were not held as scheduled in 1916, 1940, and 1944. Do you know why?

The events were cancelled in 1916 due to World War I and in 1940 and 1944 because of World War II.

Greatest Gold

Winning an Olympic gold medal remains one of sport's greatest individual achievements. Whether it is in the heat of summer for being the fastest swimmer, best gymnast, or longest jumper, or in the chill of winter for being the speediest skater or the most skilful skier, earning a gold is the peak of an athlete's career and one of the highlights of his or her life. Here are the top male and female career gold-medal winners in Olympic Games history.

ATHLETE, COUNTRY	SPORT
10 GOLD MEDALS	
Ray Ewry, United States*	Track and field
9 GOLD MEDALS	
Larissa Latynina, USSR**	Gymnastics
Carl Lewis, United States	Track and field
Paavo Nurmi, Finland	Track and field
Mark Spitz, United States	Swimming
8 GOLD MEDALS	
Matt Biondi, United States	Swimming
Bjorn Dahlie, Norway	Cross-country skiing
Kato Sawao, Japan	Gymnastics
Jenny Thompson, United States	Swimming
7 GOLD MEDALS	
Nikolay Andrianov, USSR	Gymnastics
Vera Caslavska, Czechoslovakia	Gymnastics
Birgit Fischer, Germany	Kayaking
Boris Shacklin, USSR	Gymnastics
6 GOLD MEDALS	
Aladar Gerevich, Hungary	Fencing

Medal Winners

ATHLETE, COUNTRY	SPORT
Edoardo Mangiarotti, Italy	Fencing
Neo Nadi, Italy	Fencing
Kristin Otto, Germany	Swimming
Michael Phelps, United States	Swimming
Vitaly Scherbo, Belarus	Gymnastics
Lidia Skoblikova, USSR	Speed skating

5 GOLD MEDALS

Bonnie Blair, United States	Speed skating
Krisztina Egerszegi, Hungary	Swimming
Eric Heiden, United States	Speed skating
Tom Jager, United States	Swimming
Michael Johnson, United States	Track and field
Pal Kovacs, Hungary	Fencing
Takashi Ono, Japan	Gymnastics
Steven Redgrave, Great Britain	Rowing
Ingemar Stenmark, Sweden	Alpine skiing
Johnny Weissmuller, United States	Swimming

* Two of Ray's medals came at a semi-official 1906 Olympic event.

** "USSR" stands for the Union of Soviet Socialist Republics, or Soviet Union, a nation that broke up in 1991 to become Russia and many other smaller nations.

Larissa Latynina won more Olympic medals of all types than any other athlete. Along with her nine golds, she won five silver (second place) medals, and four bronze (third place) medals from 1956 to 1964.

Arctic Games

You've heard of the Olympic Games, of course. But the Aleut and Inuit people of Canada and Alaska have been taking part in other athletic activities for generations. Different organizations hold Arctic Games every year made up of some of the wildest sports you've ever seen. Here is a list of a few of the more unusual events held at these Games.

One-foot high kick
Jumping off one foot, touch that foot as high up a pole as possible. There is also a two-foot high kick event.

Blanket toss
Perform gymnastic manoeuvres as your teammates repeatedly fling you in the air from a blanket made of walrus skins.

Ear pull
This is tug-of-war — only you pull on a cord attached to your and your opponent's ears!

Ear weight carry
Hang a 7.2 kg (16-lb.) weight from your ear and walk as far as you can.

Eskimo stick pull
Seated facing your opponent, have a tug-of-war with a short stick instead of a rope.

Greased pole walk
How far can you walk on a wooden pole covered in slippery seal grease?

Four-man carry
Four people climb on top of you and you walk as far as you can.

Kneel jump
Jump as far as you can, starting from a kneeling position.

Knuckle hop
Resting on only your knuckles and toes and with your elbows bent, hop until you can't hop anymore. The record is 57 m (191 feet)!

Indian stick pull
Using one hand, battle with your opponent for possession of a .6 m (two-foot) greased stick.

Most of the events in the Arctic Games were created to mimic things that hunters might have to do to survive in the wild. For instance, a hunter might have to carry a couple of injured partners (or a huge seal), as in the four-man carry event. The knuckle hop helped toughen up hunters' hands for hard work.

Hiiiii-YA!
Martial Arts Ranks

Most martial arts use colours to rank participants in their sports. People earn higher ranks, or colours, by learning new skills, perfecting techniques, or just whomping people at a competition. There are many different kinds of martial arts, but here are two examples of what colours are used to signify the levels or ranks.

Tae Kwan Do

(ranked from lowest to highest)

COLOUR	MEANING
White	purity, innocence
Yellow	rising sun, source of life
Green	growing things
Blue	sky, open and boundless
Red	blood, the essence of life
Black	all colours combined

Judo

(ranked from lowest to highest)

1. white
2. yellow
3. orange
4. green
5. blue
6. brown
7. black
8. red and white

Every school of martial arts has its own way of ranking. Also, martial arts from different countries use different terms. In Japanese karate, for example, each rank is called *kyu*. In Korean, those *kyus* are called *gups*. So new karate students are called "guppies."

Track-and-Field Events

Running, jumping, and throwing are the three main skills in track-and-field events. The running events are the "track" part, while the jumping and throwing make up the "field." These are the classic track-and-field events as seen every four years at the Olympic Summer Games.

Running:

100 metres

200 metres

400 metres

800 metres

1,500 metres

3,000 metres

5,000 metres

10,000 metres

Marathon

400-metre hurdles

110-metre hurdles

3,000-metre steeplechase

4x100-metre relay

4x400-metre relay

20-km walk

50-km walk

Jumping:

High jump

Long jump

Pole vault

Triple jump

Throwing:

Shot put

Discus

Hammer

Javelin

Multiple-skill events:

Heptathlon

Decathlon

The heptathlon is seven track-and-field events. It is normally done by female athletes. Male athletes tackle the ten-event decathlon. In the 1912 Olympics, the great Native American athlete Jim Thorpe won both the decathlon and a five-event pentathlon, which is no longer held.

Most Radical Skaters

And we're not talking about ice-skaters here. . . . These are the best, most successful, and most innovative skateboarders around. They do things on a skateboard that most of us can't do standing still or even bouncing on a trampoline. They are a mix of street and vert-ramp skaters, and you might see them on TV or at an arena near you. (Oh, yes, and in competition, they all always wear their helmets.)

Bob Burnquist

This Brazilian is probably best vert skater in the world.

Cara-Beth Burnside

Olympic snowboarder turned star vert skater.

Tony Hawk

Simply the world's greatest and most famous skateboarder. Among other things, the only person to pull a 900 (2½ complete spins in the air) off a vert ramp.

Bucky Lasek

Three-time X Games gold medalist.

Andy McDonald

Versatile, popular pro with 10 X Games medals.

Chad Muska

Creative and innovative street skater.

Ryan Sheckler

Radical 16-year-old 2004 X Games gold medalist.

Elissa Steamer

Top women's skater, awesome on vert ramp.

Danny Way

First skater to jump across the Great Wall of China.

Skateboards were invented in the 1950s when California surfers were looking for a way to stay in surfing shape during the off-season. They attached roller-skate wheels to wooden boards and used their surfing skills on the streets. In the 1970s, molded plastic wheels and boards changed the sport dramatically.

Ollies and Others

There are about as many skateboard tricks as there are skateboarders. You've probably made up a few of your own and given them names that will make you famous around the world . . . as soon as you can do your tricks at the X Games. Here are some names and brief descriptions of well-known skateboard tricks. It takes pros years to learn most of these, some of which can be dangerous, so **don't** try these by yourself at home!

Board slide
Ride a rail with your board and the rail forming a T. There's also a tailslide, with just the back part of the board sliding on the rail or obstacle.

Frontside 180
As you roll along, ollie (see below) and spin your body and board so that the back foot becomes the front foot.

Grab
A grab trick is any time you get air and reach down to grab the board with your hands. An indy grab is from behind, and there are also tail and nose grabs, among many others.

Grind
Ride a rail on your back wheels alone. You can nosegrind, tailgrind, or 50-50 (along one side of the board).

Kickflip
Ollie, but then spin the board around parallel to your feet.

Ollie
Kick the board tail-first off the ground and then land on it again.

Pop shove it
Ollie, but spin the board like a propeller before landing.

360
This is a vert-ramp trick; you fly off the lip and do a complete spin before landing again. A 540 is one-and-a-half spins.

You can ride a skateboard with either foot in front. If you ride with your right foot in front, you're riding "right." It's called "goofy-foot" if you ride with your left in front. Riding both ways lets you do the most tricks.

Whoa. Dude.

This list includes the most outrageous shredders . . . the most radical drop-down artists . . . the gnarliest surfers in the world! They're the bravest, the most outrageous, heck, just the coolest guys and gals around at this awesome sport. Cowabunga, dude!

Megan Abudo
Hawaii
Ranked number one in the world, 2001.

Lisa Andersen
Florida
Four-time women's world champion.

Layne Beachley
Australia
World champ in 1998, set women's record for prize money.

Serena Brooke
Australia
One of the top young surfers on the world tour.

Tim Curran
California
Talented young surfer, a future superstar.

* Association of Surfing Professionals

Shane Dorian
Australia
One of the best on the ASP* Tour.

Sunny Garcia
Hawaii
World champion in 2000, 36 ASP Tour victories.

Bethany Hamilton
Hawaii
Lost an arm in a shark attack in 2003, but continues to compete professionally.

C. J. Hobgood
Florida
World champion in 2001.

Lynette McKenzie
Australia
World number one in 2002.

Kelly Slater
California
The best surfer ever? He has won a record six world titles.

Hawaiian legend Duke Kahanamoku was one of the people most responsible for making surfing popular. A champion swimmer, his fame let him spread the word about surfing, a sport beloved by his fellow Hawaiians.

Weird World of Sports

Baseball . . . basketball . . . boring! There is much more to the wide world of sports than just the games you are used to watching and playing. We've scoured the globe to come up with a list of unusual sports that you won't see every day. Listed with each sport is a country in which it is popular.

Bungee jumping/New Zealand
A big drop from a high place on a long rubber band.

Caber tossing/Scotland
Strong men try to flip telephone poles.

Camel racing/Saudi Arabia
In other countries, people race on ostriches and elephants.

Elephant polo/Thailand
They use a huge rubber ball instead of a small hard one.

Mountain unicycling/United States
Like mountain biking, only with one wheel.

Road bowling/Ireland
Bowlers throw small metal balls along very long roads.

Sepak takraw/Thailand
A form of soccer that is played like tennis.

Sumo wrestling/Japan
Men as large as 270 kg (600 lb.) go belly to belly.

Underwater hockey/Canada
Go for the goal . . . 1.8 m (six feet) underwater!

Waterfall kayaking/Indonesia
They just keep paddling — straight down!

The sport of lacrosse is enormously popular in Canada. It was originally a game played by Aboriginal Peoples. Instead of playing on a field, however, they would play over huge areas of open land, with the goals located in neighbouring villages.

Weighty Matters

Boxing is a pretty tough sport to begin with. Imagine if a boxer the size of Bart Simpson had to take on a fighter as big as The Rock! To keep things fair, boxing has created weight classes. Before a fight, judges make sure each fighter is a legal weight for his class.

CLASS	MAXIMUM WEIGHT (KG/LB.)
Strawweight	47.5/105
Junior Flyweight	48.9/108
Flyweight	50.7/112
Junior Bantamweight	52.0/115
Bantamweight	53.4/118
Junior Featherweight	55.2/122
Featherweight	57.0/126
Junior Lightweight	58.8/130
Lightweight	61.1/135
Junior Welterweight	63.4/140
Welterweight	66.5/147
Junior Middleweight	69.7/154
Middleweight	72.4/160
Super Middleweight	76.1/168
Light Heavyweight	79.2/175
Cruiserweight	86.0/190
Heavyweight	86.5/191 and above

In April 2000, Lennox Lewis (113.2 kg/250 lb.) and Michael Grant (111.8 kg/247 lb.) squeezed into a ring for the most combined weight ever in a championship fight. Lewis smushed Grant in two rounds.

Little League World Series

Since 1947, Little League Baseball has held its world championship in Williamsport, Pennsylvania. Little League holds eight national tournaments for boys and girls in different age divisions of baseball and softball. The Little League baseball division, for 11-12 year olds, is the most famous. Beginning in 2000, 16 teams from around the world made the finals to compete for the title.

YEAR	COUNTRY or CITY, STATE	YEAR	COUNTRY or CITY, STATE
1947	Williamsport, PA	1977	Chinese Taipei
1948	Lock Haven, PA	1978	Chinese Taipei
1949	Hammonton, NJ	1979	Chinese Taipei
1950	Houston, TX	1980	Chinese Taipei
1951	Stamford, CT	1981	Chinese Taipei
1952	Norwalk, CT	1982	Kirkland, WA
1953	Birmingham, AL	1983	Marietta, GA
1954	Schenectady, NY	1984	Seoul, South Korea
1955	Morrisville, PA	1985	Seoul, South Korea
1956	Roswell, NM	1986	Chinese Taipei
1957	Mexico	1987	Chinese Taipei
1958	Mexico	1988	Chinese Taipei
1959	Hamtramck, MI	1989	Trumbull, CT
1960	Levittown, PA	1990	Chinese Taipei
1961	El Cajon/La Mesa, CA	1991	Chinese Taipei
1962	San Jose, CA	1992	Long Beach, CA
1963	Granada Hills, CA	1993	Long Beach, CA
1964	Staten Island, NY	1994	Maracaibo, Venezuela
1965	Windsor Locks, CT	1995	Chinese Taipei
1966	Houston, TX	1996	Chinese Taipei
1967	Tokyo, Japan	1997	Guadalupe, Mexico
1968	Wakayama, Japan	1998	Toms River, NJ
1969	Chinese Taipei	1999	Hirakata, Japan
1970	Wayne, NJ	2000	Sierra Maestra, Venezuela
1971	Chinese Taipei	2001	Kitasuna, Japan
1972	Chinese Taipei	2002	Louisville, KY
1973	Chinese Taipei	2003	Tokyo, Japan
1974	Chinese Taipei	2004	Willemstad, Curaçao
1975	Lakewood, NJ	2005	
1976	Chofu, Japan	2006	

More than three million youth worldwide play Little League Baseball. Canada received the first charter for a Little League team outside of the U.S. in 1951, and the first Canadian Little League champions were a team from Montreal.

Wild Wrestlers!

In the past decade, one of the most popular sports in the country has been wrestling. Some people would not call these carefully planned "fights" sports. In fact, the new name of the largest pro wrestling group is World Wrestling Entertainment. Whether they are sports or shows, these events feature stars with some pretty wild names. Here are some of the biggest names in the world of wrestling.

Kurt Angle
Stone Cold Steve Austin
Batista
Chris Benoit
John Cena
Edge
Hulk Hogan
Chris Jericho
Kane
Nitro Girls
The Rock
RVD
Trish Stratus
The Undertaker
Triple H

In the 1950s, pro wrestling was almost as big as it is today. The wrestlers, however, rarely wore bizarre costumes or engaged in wild theatrics. One who did was Gorgeous George, whose bleached blond hair and big capes helped set the stage for today's wild wrestlers.

My Sports

Okay, now you've seen how the world of pro and Olympic sports lines up. What's on your personal sports lineup?

My favourite sport to play _____

My favourite sport to watch _____

My least favourite sport _____

A sport I wish I played better _____

My favourite player in my favourite sport _____

My favourite player in another sport _____

My favourite team _____

My favourite pro sports memory _____

My school's team nickname _____

A league I play in _____

My team's name _____

My uniform number _____

Two hundred years ago, Canadian kids didn't have pro or Olympic or even high school sports teams to watch. They played games instead, including rounders, a sort of early baseball; bowls, which was like outdoor bowling; and probably good old-fashioned tag.

Index

How to Say Good-bye

Well, we've come to the last page in the book, our last list. We hope you've had some fun, learned a few things, and perhaps thought of new lists of your own. To send you off in style, this final list shows you how to say "good-bye" in 20 languages from around the world.

LANGUAGE	GOOD-BYE (HOW TO SAY IT)
Apache	Ka dish day (KAH dish day)
Chinese	Zài jiàn (ZAI-JEN)
Czech	Nashle (NAHSH-lay)
Dutch	Vaarwell (vahr-VELL)
French	Au revoir (OH-ruh-VWAH)
German	Auf wederhesen (au-VEE-der-zayn)
Greek	Yasou (YAH-soo)
Hawaiian	Aloha (ah-LOH-ha)
Hebrew	Shalom (shah-LOHM)
Hindi	Namaste (nah-mahs-TAY)
Indonesian	Daa daa (DAH dah)
Irish	Slán leat (slan LEESH)
Italian	Ciao (CHOW)
Japanese	Sayonara (sy-oh-NAH-rah)
Kiswihali	Kwaheri (kwa-HARE-ee)
Maori	E noho ra (ay no-ho RAH)
Portuguese	Até a vista (ah-TAY ah VEES-tah)
Russian	Do svidanja (dohs vee-DAN-yah)
Spanish	Adios (AH-dee-ose)
Tagalog	Paalom (pah-ah-LOHM)

 Good-bye is just one way Canadians say "so long," "farewell," "see you later," "catch you on the flip-flop," "bye-bye," and, of course, "ta-ta for now!"